SUCCESS WITH
BULBS

P9-DDZ-173

DISCARD

SUCCESS WITH
BULBS

Eric Sawford

GUILD OF MASTER CRAFTSMAN
PUBLICATIONS LTD

First published 2004 by
Guild of Master Craftsman Publications Ltd,
166 High Street, Lewes,
East Sussex BN7 1XU

Text © Eric Sawford 2004
© in the Work GMC Publications Ltd

Reprinted 2005

ISBN 1 86108 357 2

British Cataloguing in Publication Data
A catalogue record of this book is available from the British Library.

Managing Editor: Gerrie Purcell
Commissioning Editor: April McCroskie
Production Manager: Hilary MacCallum
Editors: Graham Clarke and Gill Parris
Designer: Andy Harrison
Typeface: Futura

Photographic credits:
Front cover and page 30 (top): Anthony Bailey
Most of the other photographs, including plant portraits, were taken by
Eric Sawford. The Publisher would like to thank Graham Clarke for
supplying all supplementary photographs.

Whilst every effort has been made to obtain permission from the copyright
holders for all material used in this book, the publishers will be pleased
to hear from anyone who has not been appropriately acknowledged,
and to make the correction in future reprints.

Colour origination by Icon Reproduction, London
Printed and bound by Sino Publishing House Ltd, Hong Kong, China

Contents

ABOVE **Hardy** *Cyclamen coum* **make a fine show**

RIGHT **Tulips and crown imperials**

Introduction

Gardens that have been planned and planted with care are both enjoyable and satisfying, and bulbs can provide a hugely important part. The variety of bulbous plants is enormous; nothing can surpass the range of colours available – whether vibrant or more subtle shades, the choice is endless.

Bulbs can be planted in conjunction with other garden plants, or used on their own. And bulbs should not be considered merely for a spring display – they can provide wonderful shows throughout the year, even in winter, when the delightful *Cyclamen coum* can produce a carpet of colour.

It is possible to create numerous schemes in the garden, ranging from the 'hot colours' to those of a more serene type. Take the tulip as an example: there are the dwarf types, the tall stately Darwin hybrids, and the elegant lily-flowered, parrot and fringed groups (which have among them some of the brightest shades). Every year there are new introductions to swell

the ranks, but we should not ignore the simple pleasure to be had from the purest of white tulips, which blend so perfectly with other spring-flowering plants.

Unquestionably the principal colour of spring is yellow, and to achieve this you can choose from the many forms of *Crocus* and the tremendous range of daffodils; these latter bulbous plants are most generally associated with the arrival of spring. Garden shrubs, such as *Forsythia* and *Kerria* enhance the spring yellows.

Colour combinations are extremely important. Aim for bold, colourful displays that do not clash with other plants. Choose species and cultivars that tone in well with garden features. But one important point to remember is to keep your design simple – sizeable plantings of a few colours are far better than a conflicting display of shapes and shades.

Time spent in planning is both worthwhile (in that you'll end up with a much more attractive garden), and cost-efficient (as you only then order and buy what is required, rather than buying on impulse).

AWARD OF GARDEN MERIT

Throughout this book you will see the initials AGM set after certain plants. This denotes that the plant in question has passed certain assessments carried out by experts under the auspices of the Royal Horticultural Society in Great Britain. Only plants with exceptionally good garden qualities can be awarded this special Award of Garden Merit.

SECTION 1

11

CHAPTER 1

Where to grow bulbs outdoors

For most types of garden plant – tree, shrub, perennial, bedding plant, and so on – there are really only a few places, and ways, in which you can grow them. The most obvious location is, of course, a bed or border in the garden. Secondary, perhaps, would be the various types of container in which the plants could be set (although for trees, of course, these would have to be very large).

Bulbs, however, are wonderfully versatile, and can be planted and grown in numerous places around the garden and home.

BEDS AND BORDERS

Large formal bulb displays are normally seen in parks and large gardens, while the majority of home gardeners will grow them in beds and borders also, often among hardy plants or shrubs.

You should always choose an open, sunny position or, at the least, where the bulbs will receive sun for half of the day. Beds and borders that are cloaked in shade for most of the day really are not suitable. Also, it is never a good idea to plant the bulbs in regimental lines; they will look far more natural in groups or clumps.

Spring-flowering subjects should be planted between mid-summer and mid-autumn. Daffodils make root growth early so they should be given preference. Tulips need the shortest growing time,

QUICK REFERENCE CHART
BULBS FOR THE ROCK GARDEN
Allium
Anemone
Camassia
Chionodoxa
Colchicum
Crocus
Cyclamen
Eranthis
Erythronium
Fritillaria
Galanthus
Hyacinthus
Iris (dwarf)
Muscari
Ornithogalum
Oxalis
Romulea
Scilla
Sternbergia
Tulipa

LEFT **Mixed plantings of tulips have tremendous visual impact**

QUICK REFERENCE CHART
BULBS FOR NATURALIZING
Allium
Anemone
Arum
Colchicum
Crocus
Cyclamen
Endymion
Erythronium
Fritillaria
Galanthus
Leucojum
Muscari
Narcissus
Ornithogalum
Scilla

so should be planted last; mid-autumn is ideal. In most borders spring-flowering bulbs will, once flowering is over, get in the way of the summer display. In this case it is advisable to lift the plants carefully, just as the foliage starts to turn yellow, and to replant them in another part of the garden. Alternatively, use a planting basket that is available from many bulb merchants. After flowering has finished you can simply lift the basket and replant it elsewhere to suit.

Daffodils, hyacinths and tulips are those most associated with a principal spring display. *Crocus* and other smaller bulbs can be used as edging. For the summer, dahlias, gladioli and lilies will brighten any border.

NATURALIZING IN GRASS

An area of grass where bulbs have been naturalized can be one of the finest reminders that spring has arrived. The most popular bulbs for growing in this way are daffodils and *Crocus*, although there are other dwarf bulbs that can be used.

ABOVE **Naturalized plantings of crocus are some of the most pleasing sights of spring**

One important point to remember is that the grass cannot be cut for around six to eight weeks after the bulbs have finished flowering. The bulbs must be allowed to die down naturally if they are to perform well in future years. It does mean, however, that during this time the area can look untidy, so you should 'naturalize' bulbs only in an 'informal' part of the garden where a few weeds, or a little untidiness will be acceptable. Immediately the bulbs have finished flowering, an application of a balanced fertilizer is beneficial. At this stage you should also water the area if the weather is dry. This will help the fertilizer to be taken up by the bulbs, and will assist the bulbs in their transition to the period of dormancy.

When naturalizing bulbs, creating an effect that is natural-looking is all-important. There are two ways this can be achieved. The first is by scattering bulbs and planting them where they fall. To do this you should use a bulb planter; this removes a plug of soil, which is replaced after the bulb has been inserted. This can be a long, backbreaking job. If a considerable number of bulbs are involved it is best to lift several strips of turf, set the bulbs on to the soil under the turf – at a suitable depth from the surface – and then replace the turf.

Snowdrops and winter aconites are easiest to establish while they are still in growth, perhaps after the flowers have finished, but before the leaves have died away. They are widely available in this form, referred to as being 'in the green'. Dry bulbs of both can take some time to settle down.

Bulbs can also be naturalized under deciduous trees and shrubs. *Anemone blanda* (AGM), *Scilla*, *Muscari* and others can be used. In grass areas, colchicums can provide autumn colour, but remember where you have planted them so the grass can be left uncut before they flower. Also, with these, the large leaves that follow the flowers are present throughout most of the spring.

CONTAINERS AND WINDOWBOXES

Containers can come in numerous shapes and forms, from simple decorative plastic pots, to stately, classical urns on plinths or pedestals. Outdoor vases, wooden tubs, concrete tanks, wire hanging baskets and, of course, windowboxes, all have a part to play. Growing bulbs in these sorts of containers is not difficult, as long as they are given good drainage, plenty of light, an open compost, water in dry spells and a degree of protection in any spells of severe frost.

Many early-flowering subjects are ideal for growing in containers. These can be positioned near to the house, where they are easily visible. This is especially welcome on days when weather conditions do not tempt you outside.

Many species tulips, together with varieties of the *Kaufmanniana*, *Greigii* and *Fosteriana* groups with their vibrant colours, are ideal. Also, the many forms of dwarf daffodil are splendid subjects for containers. *Crocus*, either the small Chrysanthus group or the much larger Dutch hybrids, can also be used to provide early colour.

Hyacinths, with their delightful fragrances, are magnificent in patio containers. Choose only one variety per container, as mixing leads to an uneven display – both in terms of the plants' height, and the precise times of flowering. Try to buy the largest bulbs you can afford, as this is reflected in flower size. On a warm, still, sunny spring morning you will certainly know the hyacinths are there – from their fragrance alone.

For summer container colour, many of the modern hybrid lilies can be excellent. Look for short-stemmed varieties, and those in the Asiatic and Oriental groups; the latter require lime-free

QUICK REFERENCE CHART
SPRING-FLOWERING BULBS
Allium
Arum
Camassia
Convallaria
Crocus
Erythronium
Fritillaria
Galanthus
Hyacinthus
Iris
Leucojum
Muscari
Narcissus
Scilla
Trillium
Tulipa

compost. Before you buy, you should always check the plants' height when fully grown, as some are too tall for containers. These would both look incongruous in a container, and be susceptible to wind damage. Many modern lilies have superb perfume.

Begonias, with their kaleidoscope of colours, are good container plants and the Pendula types are particularly suited to growing in high situations, such as windowboxes and hanging baskets.

ABOVE **A small trough of hyacinths, ready to burst into colour**

ABOVE **A display of Peruvian lilies (*Alstroemeria*)**

QUICK REFERENCE CHART
SUMMER-FLOWERING BULBS

Agapanthus
Alstroemeria
Camassia
Crinum
Crocosmia
Eucomis
Lilium
Ornithogalum
Ranunculus
Rhodohypoxis
Tulbaghia
Watsonia

SUMMER-FLOWERING BULBS

While the majority of bulbs grown in our gardens flower in the spring, there are a great many that bloom during the other seasons. For summer, the dahlias and gladioli are well known, and there are masses of varieties from which to choose.

Few gardens would not have space for one or two African lilies (*Agapanthus*), even if grown in a container. In summer these plants produce showy heads of blue or white flowers on strong stems. Peruvian lilies (*Alstroemeria*) are another good choice with a whole host of forms from which to choose. These are spectacular in borders with the 'Ligtu Hybrids' (AGM) widely regarded as being the hardiest.

If you wish to add an exotic touch, then the Indian shot plant (*Canna*) in its numerous forms will not disappoint. The bold leaves, some strongly variegated or tinged with bronze and purple, set off the tall stems of brilliantly coloured flowers.

Given a sheltered position, *Crinum* x *powellii* (AGM) can be left undisturbed to build up into a sizeable clump. *Camassia* is another useful genus of bulbous plants, as they flower from early summer, just after the spring bulbs have finished.

The sword-shaped foliage and slightly arching stems of *Crocosmia* look good in any border. These plants have become much more popular in recent years; many of the older varieties are still widely available. One of the most popular is the bright red 'Lucifer' (AGM). Plant *Crocosmias* in groups and leave them completely undisturbed.

Nowadays the range of stately lilies offered by bulb merchants and garden centres is almost overpowering. Given a sunny or lightly shaded spot they are usually quite happy. Again it is best to plant these in small groups of the same variety. Probably the best known are the Asiatic hybrids with their upward-facing flowers. Equally as attractive are those hybrids with trumpet-shaped blooms and the graceful lily species.

AUTUMN-FLOWERING BULBS

All too soon the summer changes to autumn, with its shorter days and cooler conditions. This is when a whole array of different bulbous plants come into their own. For example there is the lovely South African *Amaryllis belladonna*, which produces fragrant pink trumpet-shaped blooms in early autumn. This is also the time the first flowers appear on the many forms of *Nerine* – these can go on well into mid-autumn.

Cyclamen hederifolium (AGM) suddenly seems to appear after a late summer rain. Not

> **QUICK REFERENCE CHART**
> **AUTUMN-FLOWERING BULBS**
> *Amaryllis belladonna*
> *Colchicum*
> *Crocus speciosus*
> *Cyclamen*
> *Dahlia*
> *Nerine*
> *Schizostylis*
> *Sternbergia*

far behind are the colchicums, widely known as 'autumn crocus'. They flower before the foliage appears; this is something to consider as the leaves are large and grow steadily from mid-winter onwards. These plants should not be confused with the true autumn-flowering crocus, *Crocus speciosus*.

Most years the outdoor Kaffir lily (*Schizostylis*) is the last bulb to finish flowering before winter sets in. These are not plants for cold, exposed gardens, but where they are happy they will spread rapidly.

ABOVE *Colchicum autumnale* add welcome colour in the autumn. Position carefully, as they produce large foliage later

CHAPTER 2

Where to grow bulbs indoors

We have seen that bulbs can be grown outdoors in various ways. They also make excellent plants for providing colour in protected conditions. These include greenhouses (heated and unheated), conservatories and, of course, the home itself.

THE ALPINE AND COOL GREENHOUSE

Numerous bulbous plants are ideal subjects for growing with alpine and rockery plants. Indeed, many originate from mountain regions. An 'alpine house' is ideal for such plants. This may look like a greenhouse, but it is designed to

different specifications, and is used for a different purpose. Most greenhouses are used to create warm and often more humid conditions than outdoors. The alpine house, however, is constructed to be as airy as possible, whilst excluding the worst of the elements (rain and high winds predominately). Alpines houses are often completely without heating.

Growing bulbs in such a structure will necessitate you keeping them in pots. After flowering they can be moved to a cold frame or placed under the bench, and kept watered until they die back naturally.

Crocus and irises can be guaranteed to produce very early colour under glass. The former comprises many species, and the delightful Chrysanthus hybrids. Among the iris are the early-flowering lemon yellow *Iris danfordiae* that blooms in mid-winter. Also the lovely blue *Iris histrioides* and the royal purple *I. h.* 'George' (AGM). Varieties of *Iris reticulata* (AGM) are also good in a cool greenhouse; these include 'Cantab', pale blue, and 'Harmony', a uniform sky blue with a yellow central ridge. Another to try is the reddish-purple 'J.S. Dijt', its falls having orange-yellow markings. Always a source of attention is 'Katherine Hodgkin' (AGM), with its mid-winter

LEFT **An alpine house provides perfect protection for many species and cultivars of bulbs**

ABOVE *Hippeastrums* have large, fleshy bulbs

RIGHT **When in flower, *Hippeastrums* are dramatic**

cream-yellow flowers overlaid with a blend of light yellow and green-blue.

Early spring is the time for the rich blue flowers of the Chilean blue crocus, *Tecophilaea cyanocrocus* (AGM). There are two forms: 'Leichtlinii' (AGM), with blooms that are slightly paler, and containing a conspicuous white centre, and 'Violacea', best described as an intense purple-blue.

One fritillary that has become very popular in recent years and is now widely available, is the charming *Fritillaria michailovskyi* (AGM). It is an excellent subject for the alpine house, producing rounded chocolate bells tipped with bright yellow on 6in (15cm) stems in the spring. Taller and slightly later flowering is *F. uva-vulpis* (formerly *F. assyriaca*) that produces brown bells with gold, reflexed tips.

Indispensable for any collection are the dwarf cyclamen; these include some tender forms that, if subjected to severe frosts, would soon perish. One of the finest of the spring-flowering forms is *Cyclamen libanoticum* with large blush-pink flowers. Another good choice is the violet-

QUICK REFERENCE CHART
TENDER BULBS

Begonia
Canna
Clivia
Cyrtanthus
Dahlia
Gladiolus
Gloriosa
Hedychium
Hippeastrum
Hymenocallis
Lachenalia
Tigridia

carmine and fragrant *C. pseudibericum* (AGM). There are others that flower in the autumn, such as *C. africanum*, *C. cyprium* and *C. graecum*.

One bulb that originates from high altitudes in South Africa and flowers in the summer is *Rhodohypoxis baurii*. There are numerous

ABOVE **Close-up of a flame orange tuberous begonia**

LEFT **White tuberous begonias can be stunning against the green leaves**

named forms in a range of colours – mainly pinks and whites – all suitable for growing in shallow pots or pans. They make splendid subjects for an alpine or cool greenhouse.

GREENHOUSES, CONSERVATORIES AND INDOORS

Probably the most widely grown bulb for indoors is the *Hippeastrum*. It is sold widely, from nurseries and garden centres as well as general stores and supermarkets. These plants, with their flamboyant trumpet-shaped flowers, are very popular. They are not difficult to grow. Purchase them during autumn or winter, and plant them in John Innes no. 3 compost, with around half the bulb showing above the soil surface. Water them, then leave to

drain for a while, before placing in a warm, bright spot. Once the flower buds start to appear feed every two weeks with liquid tomato fertilizer, which is high in potash, and promotes flowering over root and leaf production. The flower spike is produced before the leaves start to develop. Each stem normally has three blooms, and with the larger bulbs there is often a second stem that develops as the first one goes over. Most will go on to produce four mid-green strap-shaped leaves. Dead-head as the flowers fade, keep the compost moist and feed occasionally until the foliage dies down.

Begonias are excellent under glass, as their flowers are particularly prone to damage by summer storms and heavy rain. The double-flowered tuberous begonias also have a range of brilliant colours. With these, if you remove the single female flowers positioned behind the main bud, the male double flower will be better, and it will make the plant more attractive.

'PREPARED BULBS'

For some of us it is desirable to have bulbs flowering in the home, long before they are flowering – or even emerging – in the garden.

Bulbs available for early flowering are 'prepared'; this means that they have been subjected to light and temperature conditions in the nursery, which leads them to think winter has passed and it is time to grow and flower. For this reason they are slightly more expensive. The most popular of prepared bulbs are the hyacinths. Ideally these bulbs should be 9in (23cm) or so in circumference; plant only one variety per bowl. Depending on size of the container use three or five bulbs. They can also be planted individually into smaller pots.

Hyacinths should be planted in late summer for Christmas flowering. Use John Innes no. 1, or a good soil-less (peat- or coir-based) compost. Ensure the pots have good drainage. If using containers with no drainage holes, a layer of gravel or coarse grit in the base will help. Set the bulbs with the tips just showing above the surface.

Once planted, water the bulbs well and place the bowls in a cool, dark, frost-free place for eight to ten weeks. Keep the compost moist at all times and protect the bulbs from mice, which will consider them a tasty meal. Alternatively, they can be plunged under a 6in (15cm) layer of sand in a garden frame. The cool period is required to build up a strong root system that will be necessary for forcing.

After the cool period, bring the containers into the light; the shoot growth will turn green after a few days. Then introduce them to warmth and full light to bring them into bloom. Use ordinary unprepared hyacinths for later flowering.

Other bulbs that can be treated to flower early include *Narcissus*, *Tulipa* and *Crocus*. The length of time required varies: tulips will take 12–14 weeks, narcissi require much cooler conditions before being brought inside for flowering, and crocus should be left in the dark for 12 weeks (they will still come into bloom before those growing outside).

RIGHT **Single hyacinths can be grown in small vases of water**

QUICK REFERENCE CHART
BULBS FOR CUT FLOWERS
Allium
Alstroemeria
Clivia
Crocosmia
Dahlia
Freesia
Gladiolus
Iris
Ixia
Lilium
Narcissus
Nerine
Sparaxis
Tulipa

CHAPTER 3

Buying bulbs

It is around mid-summer when the first of the new season's bulb catalogues drop through the letterbox. The range of bulbs available by mail order is more extensive than the shop-bought ranges, and includes many unusual and often rare varieties.

Although spring may seem, and is, a long way off, ordering early has many advantages. The first is that of 'dispatch': orders are sent out in strict rotation. Bulbs that require early planting, such as colchicums and daffodils, will be with you in good time. The second advantage of early ordering is that some varieties may be sold out later in the season. This applies particularly to new varieties, which may have been promoted heavily in gardening magazines or on television: these are always the most popular varieties and run out of stock first.

ABOVE **There are many mail order companies specializing in bulbs**

Bulbs will also be on display at garden centres from mid-summer onwards, offering the purchaser the opportunity to browse, choose, and plan a display. Much useful information on colour, height and growing is to be found on accompanying promotional material. If you have any questions do not be afraid to ask a member of the staff.

LOOK FOR QUALITY

There are a number of important points to remember when buying bulbs. Avoid any that do not have a clean base. Avoid any that are soft, or which show any sign of rot. Avoid also any that have started to shoot, or that have produced more than a very small amount of growth. This applies

LEFT **When buying bulbs, avoid any that show signs of rot**

ABOVE **Bulbs are often sold in large garden centre 'bins'**

RIGHT **Lily bulbs should be fleshy and firm**

especially to daffodils and hyacinths. Select plump, firm, well-rounded examples.

Lily bulbs should be fleshy and firm, and avoid any that appear to have dried out.

Prepared hyacinths for Christmas flowering should be purchased and planted by late summer. These will be slightly more expensive. It is generally the case that the larger the bulb, the better the flower spikes.

During the spring months you will find for sale many of the bulbs and tubers for flowering in summer. Among these are dahlias, lilies and gladioli. Always check their condition before buying, and if you are buying loose tubers from large, open boxes in a shop, write the name and colour of the variety on the bag, as a reminder.

If you are buying daffodils for naturalizing, you will probably want a relatively large quantity, and for this reason you can often buy them by weight in nets, or by quantity of bulbs (25, 50, 75, and so on). These will be of suitable varieties, often a mixture of varieties, and will be set at a competitive price. Alternatively, you can usually make your own selection of varieties from large bins. Plant out the daffodils as soon as

possible after purchasing, and do not forget to label the spot, to avoid any later accidental damage to the growing shoots.

If you have to store bulbs for long periods of time prior to planting, keep them in a cool, dry place, and never near to heaters. Do not store them in plastic bags, because this can cause rotting. Open storage bags a while before planting, to allow air to circulate around the bulbs.

RIGHT **Bulbs for naturalizing are sold in large nets**

CHAPTER 4

Growing bulbs

Now that you have bought your bulbs – from the garden centre or specialist bulb supplier, you need to know, in general terms, what to do with them. In this chapter therefore we will be looking at all of the main requirements for growing healthy bulbs, from planting to flowering splendour.

In the A–Z directory of bulbs that follows this chapter, specific growing requirements for individual bulb types are given under the relevant plant headings.

BELOW **Bulbs can be planted in containers ...**

RIGHT **... or they can be naturalized in grass**

SOIL PREPARATION

One of the most important things to remember is that, whatever type of bulb you are growing, it must have a well-drained soil; waterlogged conditions will soon lead to rotting. Well worked soil that has had rotted manure or compost incorporated for previous plants is best. Never plant bulbs in soil that has been newly manured, as the acidity in the manure will effectively 'burn' the young roots and shoots of the emerging bulbs. If your soil contains a high proportion of clay, incorporating plenty of coarse grit, leaf mould or peat will improve it.

ABOVE **Daffodils are the most common bulbs for naturalizing**

PLANTING BULBS

Some people may be allergic to handling daffodil, tulip and hyacinth bulbs; these bulbs are known to cause a rash on the skin, so if in doubt, use gloves.

A great many gardeners are confused over how deep to plant bulbs. This is the best general guide to follow: a bulb should be planted so that there is the same depth of soil above it, as the depth of the bulb itself. Exceptions are bluebells and daffodils, which should be planted at twice their own depth.

WHEN TO PLANT

Most summer-flowering bulbs are planted in the spring, but beware – not all of them are hardy, such as gladiolus. By the time growth appears above soil level the danger of frost is usually

ABOVE **In borders it is best to space bulbs by hand**

ABOVE **Plant individual bulbs using an ordinary garden trowel**

25

NATURALIZING BULBS

ABOVE **1.** Small numbers of bulbs can be planted where they land

ABOVE **2.** With large numbers of bulbs, first remove a strip of turf

ABOVE **3.** Many small (*Crocus*) bulbs may be planted ...

ABOVE **4.** ... or a smaller number of larger (daffodil) bulbs

ABOVE **5.** The ultimate reward is when the naturalized bulbs come into bloom

LILIES IN POTS

ABOVE 1. Lily bulbs should be plump and firm

ABOVE 2. Ensure there is adequate drainage

ABOVE 3. The bases of the bulbs should be in contact with the soil

ABOVE 4. Fill the rest of the pot with good quality compost

passed. Lilies are hardy so can be set out in the autumn without worrying whether they will make it through the winter unscathed.

The autumn-flowering bulbs, such as *Colchicum*, autumn crocus, *Sternbergia* and *Schizostylis*, should be planted in late spring or early summer. Daffodils and *Narcissus* should be planted in late summer or the beginning of autumn, as they produce roots early. The majority of bulbs, with the exception of tulips, can be planted as soon as the summer bedding has been removed or when the ground is vacant. In the case of tulips, from mid-autumn onwards; if they are planted too early any emerging new growth may be damaged by frost.

HOW TO PLANT

Most gardeners prefer to use a trowel for planting. There are special graduated bulb trowels available, which have long, narrow blades with measurements marked on the sides making it easier to determine the correct depth.

Always ensure that the base of the bulb is in contact with the ground. Air pockets underneath can result in the roots failing to develop properly.

Unless you are planning formal beds, always plant in groups; this is much more effective, and pleasing to the eye.

If you are planting in grass, a handheld bulb planter is helpful. This is pushed into the ground, and on extraction brings with it a plug of soil.

The bulb is then inserted into the hole and the plug replaced – it is a much quicker method where large numbers of bulbs are involved.

MAINTENANCE

Bulbs, like every other kind of garden plant, need routine maintenance to keep them in tip-top condition. They are, however, among the easiest of any kind of plant to grow, so this 'maintenance' is relatively small.

FEEDING

Bulbs used for annual bedding displays do not require feeding; when they are in active growth all you need to do is to keep the soil moist.

Those bulbs that are to remain in the soil for several years will require feeding after flowering has finished, to enable them to build up reserves for the following year. Feed with a good liquid or granular fertilizer until the foliage starts to die down naturally.

LEFT **A bulb planter removes a core of soil**

DEAD-HEADING

Remove the old flowers, as soon as they have started to fade. By doing this you will be preventing the plant from setting seed, and wasting energy. This will help to ensure better or more flowers the following year.

The only exception to this is if you are wanting the plants to produce seed so that you can propagate from them this way.

DIE-BACK

When flowering has finished you should allow the leaves to die back naturally. In the case of daffodils and narcissi do not cut down or tie the leaves into neat bundles, as this can restrict the flow of the end-of-season goodness, from the leaves back down in to the bulb. In fact, this is the way that the plants store essential substances in their undergound organs. They use up a great deal of energy in flowering, and through photosynthesis the foliage replenishes it.

TO LIFT, OR NOT TO LIFT?

Of course there are the really hardy bulbs, that can stay outdoors all winter long (such as *Crocus*, *Narcissus*, *Tulipa*, *Scilla*, and so on),

ABOVE *Gladiolus* **corms being planted**

ABOVE **Spacing tulips apart in a container**

ABOVE **Remove flowers as soon as they fade**

ABOVE **Allow leaves to die down naturally**

and then there are the tender subjects that will be killed off in frosty conditions (like *Begonia*, *Gladiolus*, *Gloriosa*, *Tigridia*, and so on). Before you plant any bulbs, you should know whether they are hardy or tender, and your whole maintenance of them will revolve around this knowledge. Some gardeners prefer to lift tulips every year after they have finished flowering. This means that space is made available for summer plants, but the main reason is that it is usually considered that the bulbs are never as good the second year.

Generally it is only really necessary to lift and divide clumps of bulbs when they become crowded. Failure to do this will eventually cause the number of flowers produced to diminish. Take care when lifting bulbs (whether for storage or division) not to damage them in any way.

PROPAGATING BULBS

Many bulbs will multiply naturally and can simply be increased by division in the dormant period. Some of the offsets may take a year or so to reach flowering size.

SCALES

Lilies vary; many can be propagated by removing individual scales from the outside of the bulb. Plant these upright, in a mixture of one part peat to three parts coarse sand. In due course they should produce bulblets at the base. When these appear you can transplant them into their own individual pots.

Aerial bulbils are produced in the leaf axis of some lily species. These can be carefully collected and potted up. Others, meanwhile, produce offsets at the base of the stem; these can be carefully detached, potted up and grown on until they are ready to plant out, flowering in two or three years.

TUBERS

Dahlias can be increased by dividing the tubers. In order to grow, each piece of tuber must have a growth point, known as a bud, or eye. Some growers prefer to pot the tubers up in early spring, keeping them in a warm and moist place, such as a heated greenhouse. When the new shoots grow, these can be used as soft cuttings. When they are well rooted they should be potted up and grown on until it is time to plant them, after the danger of frost has passed.

ABOVE **Some bulbs produce offsets**

ABOVE Daffodils lifted after flowering should be dried thoroughly before storing

CORMLETS

Some bulbs, including *Crocus*, *Crocosmia* and *Gladiolus*, produce a mass of tiny cormlets, often referred to as 'spawn'. These can be collected, planted in a tray of John Innes no. 1 compost and grown on. When they are of a size to handle easily, they should be planted in nursery rows until they are big enough to plant out as mature bulbs. Flowering size is normally reached in three to four years.

ABOVE Some pests can be controlled by washing bulbs in warm, soapy water after lifting

LEFT When lifting bulbs, be careful not to damage them

SEED

Propagating bulbs by seed can be fun, but it is a lengthy process; it is usually recommended for smaller subjects only, such as *Anemone*, *Chionodoxa*, *Cyclamen* and *Scilla*. It can take as long as five years for some of these bulbs to reach flowering size. However, if you sow some bulb seeds each year, to raise different species, then once you get started, you will have a succession of stages from newly sown seed through to developing bulbs, and finally bulbs of flowering size.

If you collect your own seed, either sow straight away or store the seed until autumn or spring, bearing in mind that bulb seeds tend to germinate at the time the plant naturally emerges through the soil.

Sow autumn-, winter- and spring-flowering bulbs in autumn; the seeds will then be subjected to a period of cold, which can be beneficial to germination. You will find that some species will germinate in the autumn, whilst others will last until spring.

Sow summer-flowering bulbs in spring, and they will germinate in summer.

Use a loam-based seed compost, such as John Innes, and sow seeds thinly. It is advisable to leave new bulbs to develop in the same container for at least a whole year before moving them on. Sown seed of hardy bulbs should be kept outside, or in a cold frame, to benefit from the cold weather. Once germination begins, move outside the pots that are under cover.

Feed the seedlings with a weak solution of fertilizer, and keep the pots moist until foliage shows signs of dying down in summer (or late autumn for summer-flowering bulbs). When the leaves have died down, allow the pots to dry out a little, but not completely – as you would with mature bulbs – because the tiny bulbs can shrivel. Start watering again when signs of new growth are visible.

When the seedlings are large enough, pot them on (during a dormant period). Tip out the

ABOVE **Some lilies can be grown from scales**

ABOVE **Start dahlia tubers off in trays of sand**

ABOVE *Gladiolus* **corms produce offsets, for separating**

ABOVE **Some bulbs can be grown from seed**

ABOVE **Keep pots of ungerminated seeds outdoors**

ABOVE **Lily seedlings ready for potting up**

whole container and separate the bulbs. Then repot them individually in fresh compost, and grow these on for two or three seasons, until they are large enough to be planted out.

PESTS AND DISEASES

Unlike roses, fuchsias and vegetables, bulbous plants are relatively problem-free. But they are not totally immune to the predations of fungi, insects, molluscs and viruses.

APHIDS

The most likely pest to be encountered is the aphid – greenfly and blackfly. These should be dealt with as soon as seen, as they can carry and transmit virus diseases. Use a systemic insecticide recommended for the control of aphids, and repeat the spraying every three to four weeks (so as to catch new infestations that have flown in, as well as any adult aphids that have emerged from the egg stage – which may not have been affected by the previous chemical treatments).

MOLLUSCS

Slugs and snails occasionally attack young growths, especially in spring, and dahlias and lilies are particularly attractive to these pests. There are many supposed controls for slugs, some of which work, but the modern approach, and one which has been accepted by many organic gardeners, is the nematode control that you water on to the soil where slugs are present. The little nematodes eat into the slugs and it is an effective control. Pellets and baits are equally effective, but this means using poisonson the ground, which many people prefer not to do.

ABOVE **Aphids should be dealt with as soon as they are seen**

ABOVE **Slugs are a common pest**

EARWIGS

Dahlia growers are often faced with another troublesome pest, the earwig. It works at night, causing twisted and distorted flowers, and holes in the foliage. One method of control is to place a small inverted flowerpot filled with dry grass near to any damaged plant. The earwigs will shelter in them during the day. You can then check them daily and dispose of any found.

THRIPS

Gladioli can be attacked by thrips; this results in a streaking and flecking of both flowers and foliage. If seen, spray immediately with a contact insecticide. Attacks are usually worse in hot dry conditions.

LILY BEETLES

A pest that is on the increase is the small, bright scarlet lily beetle. Adults and their larvaefeed on leaves and stems. Keep a careful watch and remove by hand any that you see. Destroy them, as they will soon increase in numbers if left. Spraying with a contact insecticide is also beneficial. It is important to clean up around plants in autumn, as the beetles overwinter in any debris.

RODENTS

Mice and squirrels will dig up and eat small bulbs – crocus, snowdrops, gladioli and even tulips are most at risk. The rodents will also chew at both the foliage and flowers of growing plants. Trapping is the best form of control.

QUICK REFERENCE CHART
BULBS THAT CAN CAUSE AN ALLERGIC SKIN REACTION ON SOME PEOPLE
Amaryllis
Colchicum
Convallaria
Crinum
Cyclamen
Eranthis
Fritillaria
Galanthus
Hyacinthoides
Hyacinthus
Narcissus
Tulipa

VIRAL AND FUNGAL DISEASES

There are a number of viral diseases that can attack bulbs, causing yellowing of the foliage, streaking, distortion and wilting. There is no cure for these ailments, so you should dig up and burn any infected plants.

Similarly there are several fungal diseases, and some have no known cure. Here again, dig up and burn any infected plants. Powdery mildew, which is seen as a white powdery coating on the leaves, stems and (in severe cases) the flowers of some bulbs, can be treated with a systemic fungicide.

ABOVE **There are many types of slug that attack our garden plants**

CHAPTER 5

A–Z directory of bulbs

Before we examine the vast array of bulbous plants we can grow, it is perhaps a good time to clear up some of the confusion that surrounds the three groups of plants that come into the 'bulbous' category: these are 'bulbs' (of course), 'corms' and 'tubers'.

Bulbs, such as *Narcissus*, are composed of fleshy modified leaves enclosing an embryo flower – so when you buy a bulb you can almost guarantee that it will flower.

Corms and tubers are also often described as 'bulbs', and this is where the confusion starts. Whereas all three types are storage organs, containing a supply of water and food that keeps the plant alive while it is dormant, most corms and tubers are also modified, swollen stems, with the new growths coming from buds on the tops of the organs. A typical corm is that of the *Crocus*, and a tuber is that of the *Cyclamen*.

Also, confusion arises over the fact that the tubers of some plants, such as the *Dahlia*, are actually swollen roots – the tuber itself being unable to produce new growth.

Throughout the directory section of this book references will be made to all three types of bulbous plant.

AGAPANTHUS SPECIES

NAME: *AGAPANTHUS* (AFRICAN LILY)
FAMILY: **ALLIACEAE**

Description: These are splendid plants for summer colour; they are successful in borders and also ideal subjects for a large container alongside a path or on the patio. Native to South Africa, in time they form compact clumps. The roots are fleshy and require protection in cold districts

Popular species and varieties: Among the best-known members of this family are the 'Headbourne Hybrids'. The colours vary from deep violet to pale blue, and the flowers are held on stout stems of around 24–30in

ABOVE *Agapanthus* 'Profusion'

(60–75cm) high. These hybrids are generally hardier than the species.

One *Agapanthus* that never fails to attract attention when in full bloom is the pale blue *A. campanulatus* subsp. *patens* (AGM). As with all members of this family it hates root disturbance; once planted it is best left alone. It will, in time, build into a sizeable clump, with mauve flowers. Another good choice is *A. campanulatus* 'Isis' with large rounded lavender-blue flower heads in mid-summer.

Agapanthus have strap-shaped mid-green foliage. Some are deciduous, others evergreen. There are a number of species available, with a host of cultivars and hybrids. While varieties have flowers of varying shades of blue, those with pure white blooms should not be forgotten. Among the best is 'Polar Ice', with fine heads held on strong stems 39in (100cm) high

LEFT *Agapanthus campanulatas* subsp. *patens* produces showy heads of blue flowers

ABOVE *Allium giganteum*: huge flower heads on sturdy stems

Where to grow: Choose a sheltered spot in full sun, or grow your *Agapanthus* bulbs in a large tub that can be moved around the garden as required. Remember also that the *Agapanthus* is ideal for the cold greenhouse or conservatory

How to grow: The soil you use should be humus-rich, and well drained. Incorporating plenty of well-rotted compost is beneficial when preparing the site. Water well in periods of hot dry weather. Plant in the spring with the crown 2in (5cm) below ground level

Flowering period: Mid- to late summer

Maintenance: During the growing season give an occasional application of a fertilizer high in potash, to plants in beds and borders. Those grown in containers should be fed every two weeks when the plants are growing. Staking is not required. Remove dead foliage from the deciduous species in autumn, and cover the crowns of the plants with a layer of straw to protect them during the winter

Propagation: Carefully divide the fleshy roots in early to mid-spring, replant immediately. *Agapanthus* can be grown from seed, but this is a slow process – it can take several years for them to reach flowering size

Pests and diseases: Generally trouble-free

NAME: *ALLIUM* (ORNAMENTAL ONION)
FAMILY: ALLIACEAE

Description: These plants are extremely useful for bridging the gap between the spring-flowering bulbs and summer hardy perennials. Among them are some very spectacular tall and stately plants, with large flower heads composed of a huge number of small starry blooms. Others, meanwhile, are much smaller. Then, if you add to the mix the fact that they are hardy, and undemanding, it is easy to see why their popularity is increasing

ABOVE *Allium christophii*: the heads can also be dried and used in flower arrangements

Popular species and varieties: One *Allium* that is a 'must' for most gardens is *A. christophii* (AGM), sometimes referred to as the 'Star of Persia' (and also by its old Latin name of *A. albopilosum*). It grows to 18in (45cm) in height, with strap-shaped glaucous, grey-green foliage. The large rounded flower head, which can be 6in (15cm) or more across, is made up of star-shaped silvery-pink blooms. They appear from mid- to late spring.

This is also the time when *A. karataviense* (AGM) produces its white flower heads, slightly smaller than *A. christophii*, on sturdy 8in (20cm) high stems.

By contrast the drumstick flower (*A. sphaerocephalon*) has much smaller, round, compact flower heads of purple-crimson on 20in (50cm) stems in late spring. If you are looking for something different, then *A. schubertii* with huge heads of bright rose-red individual tubular blooms on long pedicels in

early summer will not disappoint. Unquestionably impressive are the densely packed 6in (15cm) wide violet flower heads of *A. giganteum* (AGM) in early summer, particularly when planted in groups. This is a native of the Himalayas and reaches 43in (110cm) in height. Another to look out for is 'Globemaster' (AGM); the enormous violet heads are 8in (20cm) or more across and produced on strong stems.

The heads of *A. cernuum* are rose-pink, on 15in (38cm) tall stems, with the individual blooms bending downwards. Ideal for naturalizing is *A. moly* (AGM), sometimes referred to as golden garlic. Growing to just 10in (25cm) in height, and flowering from mid- to late spring, it is a good plant for growing in grass, as well as for edging the front of a border. When growing in grass, it must be in a place where mowing can be left until the foliage has died back.

39

One that must not be overlooked is *A. caeruleum* (AGM) with its fine neat compact heads of deep cornflower blue on sturdy 24in (60cm) stems in late spring and early summer.

There are a great many other forms of *Allium*, most of which are readily available

Where to grow: Alliums are sun lovers; the taller types are ideal for beds and borders. The low-growing varieties can be planted on a rock garden

How to grow: Planting should take place in late summer or early autumn. As a general rule you should cover the bulbs with around three times their own depth of soil. They are most effective when planted in groups, and when left undisturbed for several years. Only after a time, when flowering becomes reduced, should they be lifted and divided. The tallest alliums may need support, especially if grown in a windy position

Flowering period: From mid-spring to early summer

Maintenance: Support taller varieties if necessary. When the flowers have finished, remove the heads and leave the stem to die back naturally (which will help to feed the bulb). In late summer remove all dead foliage and flower stems. A fortnightly application of a high potash liquid fertilizer is beneficial while buds are forming and in flower. Water alliums in dry weather

Propagation: Carefully lift and divide in the autumn; replant immediately. Many can also be grown from seed; it takes some time for them to reach flowering size

Pests and diseases: Slugs can attack young foliage. There are fungal diseases that can attack alliums: white rot results in yellow foliage and die-back, and the bulb becomes covered in a white fluffy fungal growth; rust produces orange spots on the leaves. In both cases lift and destroy the entire plants

LEFT *Allium sphaerocephalon*: the Drumstick allium

ABOVE *Alstroemerias*: available in a range of colours

NAME: *ALSTROEMERIA* (PERUVIAN LILY)
FAMILY: **ALSTROEMERIACEAE**

Description: *Alstroemerias*, with their clusters of delicately marked flowers, add a touch of the exotic to any sheltered border. They produce fleshy tubers and dark green sword-like leaves. These plants originate from South America; not all are reliably hardy. They are widely used by flower arrangers and florists. They last a long time in water if picked when the buds are just starting to open

Popular species and varieties: There are several species, but it is the hybrids that are mostly seen in our gardens. Look out for the 'Ligtu Hybrids' that are widely regarded as being among the hardiest. They are available in a wide range of colours, including scarlet, flame, orange and yellow, together with salmon pink and white

There is a range of excellent hybrids with 'Princess' in the name: these grow up to 54in (135cm) and, once established, each plant

41

produces a number of stems. Look for the golden yellow 'Princess Sophia', orange 'Princess Frederika' and rose-pink 'Princess Alice'. New varieties are always being added to the range, and two of the most recent additions are the bicoloured 'Princess Phoebe' and rich red 'Princess Rubinia'

Ideal for smaller gardens are the 'Little Princess' range, growing to just 12–16in (30–40cm). The best include 'Princess Camilla' with white, attractively marked flowers, and 'Princess Sara', an orange bicolour. Look out also for the deep red 'Princess Oxana'. 'The Golden Jubilee Lily' is a lovely pure glowing amber, just 12in (30cm) high, named by Her Majesty the Queen at Chelsea Flower Show in 2002, to celebrate her Golden Jubilee

Where to grow: Sheltered borders, protected from the worst of the wind. These plants are happy in a sunny or lightly shaded place. Choose a position where they can remain undisturbed for several years

How to grow: Well-drained humus-rich soil; alstroemerias will not tolerate cold, waterlogged conditions. The tubers are fleshy and can be damaged easily during handling. Plant in groups during spring, at a depth of 6in (15cm). Take care not to let the tubers dry out before planting. They sometimes fail to flower in their first season from tubers, so it is advisable to purchase container-grown plants, which establish quicker. Once established they are vigorous, so position with care

Flowering period: Early to mid-summer

Maintenance: It can sometimes be necessary to provide twiggy sticks as support. Water clumps well in hot, dry weather. Remove faded flowers as required. In the autumn cut the old foliage and stems (after they have died back) to ground level. In cold districts a mulch of leaf mould or peat will provide some winter protection

Propagation: Lift and carefully divide clumps in the spring; take care not to damage the tubers, replant immediately

Pests and diseases: Slugs and snails can attack young growth in the spring; early protection pays dividends. There is a virus that causes stunting, together with yellow or mottled foliage; destroy any plants showing symptoms

NAME: *AMARYLLIS* (CAPE BELLADONNA, JERSEY LILY)
FAMILY: **AMARYLLIDACEAE**

This should not be confused with the tender *Hippeastrum*, which is sold by the thousand as an 'indoor plant', and which is often referred to as *Amaryllis*. The true *Amaryllis* consists of a single species and is very different in appearance. A native of South Africa it can be grown outdoors in mild districts and should, ideally, be given protection

Popular species and varieties: *Amaryllis belladonna* flowers in late summer and early autumn, at a time when colour is particularly welcome, and when many of the hardy plants are well past their best. Up to six fragrant, rich pink, funnel-shaped blooms on strong stems – 24in (60cm) or more in height – appear before the foliage. There are several named forms mostly in shades of pink or carmine with the exception of 'Hathor' a pure white; these are usually available from specialist bulb suppliers

Where to grow: Plant in mild districts only, at the foot of a sunny wall, in a sheltered position. Amaryllis are sun lovers, requiring as much warmth and summer baking as possible; this will promote the formation of flower buds

How to grow: The soil should be well drained. Prepare the site in advance by digging in well-rotted compost. Plant in early to mid-summer with the neck of the bulb just above ground level, ideally in a clump with the bulbs spaced 8–12in (20–30cm) apart. These can be left for several years undisturbed, and in time they

RIGHT *Amaryllis belladonna*: flowers in the autumn

will form a sizeable clump, with the best flowering from well-established plantings. The glossy strap-shaped leaves start into growth after the flowers have finished; these remain until the following summer. It is important that the foliage is protected from frost as, if damaged, can lead to loss of vigour

Flowering period: Late summer to early autumn

Maintenance: Winter protection is very important. Well-established plants should be given a light dressing of a high-potash fertilizer in the autumn. Water the plants during the growth period when the weather is hot. Remove dead flowers and stems

Propagation: Carefully lift the bulbs in early summer, divide and replant immediately

Pests and diseases: Usually trouble-free

NAME: *ANEMONE* (WINDFLOWER)
FAMILY: **RANUNCULACEAE**

Description: Well-established groups of *Anemone blanda* growing at the base of a tree, or when naturalized, are a joy to behold in the spring, with the well-known *A. coronaria*, ideal for the border, flowering a few weeks later

Popular species and varieties: *Anemone blanda* (AGM) is a native of Greece and Turkey, and is available in shades of blue, pink and also white. Growing to just 6in (15cm) in height, it has open, daisy-like flowers, the first of which, in mild seasons, can appear even in

BELOW *Anemone* 'Hollandia': very distinctive flowers of bright scarlet with a boss of black stamens

ABOVE *Anemone* 'Sylphide': grow in a sheltered, well-drained spot

mid-winter. It is normally at its best in early spring. Often sold in a mixture, there are several named varieties available, including 'Radar' (AGM) a striking bright magenta with a white eye; 'Charmer', a clear pink; and 'White Splendour', with large, pure white flowers.

For many years *Anemone coronaria* has been grown in our gardens, mainly as two strains descended from this species – the De Caen and St Brigid mixtures. The former is occasionally referred to as the Poppy Anemone. Colours for both forms range from deep blue and purple, through to red, pink and white. The St Brigids come in semi- or double-flowering forms. Several named varieties are available, including the single dazzling scarlet 'Hollandia', blue-flowered double 'Lord Lieutenant', the magenta double 'Sylphide' and single pure white 'The Bride'. All the coronaria anemones are good as cut flowers. The white Wood Anemone, *A. nemorosa* (AGM), is ideal for naturalizing under trees and shrubs

Where to grow: In its natural habitat
A. blanda is found in mountain districts.
It is happy in a sunny or lightly shaded spot.
A. coronaria is a sun lover and ideal for the
front of beds and borders. *A. nemorosa* is best
under deciduous trees, ideally where it receives
sun in the morning and shade later

How to grow: Anemones enjoy humus-rich,
well-drained soil. Soaking the tubers overnight
in tepid water will assist them to become
established quickly. *A. blanda* should be
planted in the autumn, some 2in (5cm) deep
and 4in (10cm) apart. *A. coronaria* can be
planted 2in (5cm) deep in the autumn for
spring flowering, or early spring for summer
blooming; space all of the bulbs at distances
4–6in (10–15cm) apart

Flowering period: *A. blanda* blooms in early
spring, *A. coronaria* produces its flowers at
various times, depending on when the bulbs
were planted, and *A. nemorosa* flowers
throughout the spring

Maintenance: Water in dry weather, until
foliage dies back. *A. blanda* and *A. nemorosa*
will self-seed. A top-dressing of well-rotted leaf
mould applied in the winter is beneficial

Propagation: Lift and divide the tubers in late
summer. Sow seed as soon as it is ripe; it will
normally take one to two years before they are
ready for planting out

Pests and diseases: Several virus diseases
can cause distortion and mottling of the
foliage; any plants affected should be dug up
and destroyed

LEFT *Anemone* 'White Splendour': large, showy snow-white flowers

NAME: *BEGONIA*
FAMILY: **BEGONIACEAE**

Description: These are great favourites for providing summer colour, with the large-flowered varieties being excellent for pots in the conservatory, windowboxes or patio containers. They can also be used for bedding out but not before all danger of frost has passed. The pendulous varieties are excellent for growing in hanging baskets

Popular species and varieties: There are a considerable number of begonia flower forms – single, double, some with heavily ruffled petals,

also camellia- and carnation- flowered varieties (often listed as *B. x tuberhybrida*). Among the most popular forms are 'Bouton de Rose' with double, well-formed blooms of pink edged with white, and 'Marmorata', its carmine flowers are marbled with white, and the petals of which are ruffled and waved. The graceful pendulous

begonias produce a large number of flowers over a long period. Many begonias are also frequently offered by colour only

Where to grow: Tuberous begonias are not hardy. If planting outside, this should not be before the late spring. They can be used for bedding, patio containers and window boxes. The pendulous begonias look good in hanging baskets or wherever the long trailing foliage and flowers can be seen to best effect

How to grow: Start the tubers into growth in the spring in boxes containing peat. Place them in the peat without covering, and with the hollow side uppermost. When growth starts, pot them up individually, and grow them on. Place them in a garden frame or unheated greenhouse, and gradually harden them off before planting them out. Once flowering has finished they should be lifted before the first frosts of autumn. A light, well-drained humus-rich soil is essential, in a sunny or lightly shaded spot that is sheltered from the wind. During the summer feed every two weeks with a high-potash liquid fertilizer

Flowering period: Summer through to early autumn

Maintenance: Remove dead flower heads. Lift the tubers as they start to die down in the autumn. Dry, clean, and store them for the winter in a frost-free place in dry peat

Propagation: Tuberous begonias can be increased by stem cuttings taken in early spring. Root the cuttings in an equal mix of coarse sand and peat. When well rooted, pot up the young plants individually, and grow them on

Pests and diseases: Powdery mildew can cause problems. Treat plants and tubers with a suitable fungicide. Vine weevils can attack plants in pots and containers; treat the compost with a pesticide, or use natural predators

LEFT *Begonia* x *tuberhybrida*: splendid for containers and window boxes

NAME: *CAMASSIA* (QUAMASH)
FAMILY: **HYACINTHACEAE**

Description: Camassias are native to North America. They are handsome plants for the border in good moisture-retentive soil. The tall stems carry numerous closely packed star-shaped flowers. Once planted, leave the plants undisturbed for several years to steadily build up into sizeable clumps

Popular species and varieties: One of the best known is *C. leichtlinii* subsp. *suksdorfii*, a reliable plant with 36in (90cm) high flowering stems, carrying blue flowers. *C. leichtlinii subsp. leichtlinii* (also sometimes found as 'Alba') produces attractive white flowers. The Caerulea group has deep mauve-blue flowers. *C. cusickii* is widely available; this grows to 20in (50cm), and its flowers are a silvery-blue over a rosette of broad glaucous foliage. *Camassia quamash* (sometimes listed as *C. esculenta*) grows to around 24in (60cm). The flowers range in colour from blue and purple to white

Where to grow: These bulbous plants are ideal subjects for a border; their early flowering makes them invaluable, as most hardy perennials will be just starting into growth

How to grow: Camassias are happy in full sun or light shade. They enjoy cool, moist humus-rich conditions but not where they can become waterlogged. Plant in early to mid-autumn, 4in (10cm) deep and 6in (15cm) apart

Flowering period: Mostly early summer

Maintenance: Water well in hot, dry conditions. On poor soils an application of a good general fertilizer applied in the spring, and carefully worked in to the soil, is beneficial. Cut down the flower stems when the blooms have faded. They are best left undisturbed for several years, so mark the spot to avoid accidental damage when the bulbs are dormant

Propagation: Carefully lift and divide in the autumn; replant immediately

Pests and diseases: Normally trouble-free

ABOVE *Camassia cusickii*: leave undisturbed to build up into clumps

NAME: *CANNA* (INDIAN SHOT)
FAMILY: **CANNACEAE**

Description: Bold, dramatic, architectural plants for containers or the border, they are exotic-looking with brilliantly coloured flowers that you can hardly fail to miss. They form rhizomes and are not hardy; when used for summer bedding they should be started under cover and planted out when the danger of frosts has passed

Popular species and varieties: Most of those grown today are hybrids. 'Black Knight' has dark red flowers with wavy petals; each flower is held well clear of the attractive purple-bronze foliage. It grows to 60in (150cm), making it

an ideal subject for the centre of a bed. The lemon yellow 'Richard Wallace' is not as tall, reaching 40in (100cm)

One that is certainly eye-catching is 'Picasso', the blue-green leaves being a perfect foil for the yellow blooms that are heavily spotted with red. This differs from the others in that it is best grown in a lightly shaded spot where its blooms on 45in (120cm) stems can be seen at their best. Another one not to overlook is 'Wyoming', its brown-purple leaves are attractive in their own right. The orange flowers have an apricot feathering

There are lower-growing varieties ideal for patio containers and smaller gardens. One of these is 'Delibab', which grows to just 16in (40cm), with orange-red flowers over bronzy foliage. The old rose-pink variety 'Orchid' is slightly taller

Where to grow: Most cannas are suitable for the centre of a bed, or in the border. Dwarf varieties are ideal for containers

How to grow: In the early spring start the rhizomes into growth in peat, in a frost-free greenhouse. Plant outside in early summer. Alternatively place rhizomes 3in (7.5cm) deep in a good humus-rich well-drained soil when the danger of frost has passed. In cold districts grow them in tubs that can be moved outside in mid-summer

With the exception of 'Picasso' (which is best in a lightly shaded spot), cannas are sun lovers. Water plants well in hot dry weather. Feed with a high-potash liquid fertilizer when the flower buds begin to develop

Flowering period: Summer into early autumn

Maintenance: Cut down dead flower stems. Lift and dry the rhizomes in the early autumn. Store the rhizomes over the winter in a frost-free place in slightly moist peat, to prevent them becoming too dry

LEFT *Canna* 'Picasso': this variety is best in partial shade

RIGHT *Canna* 'Wyoming': dramatic purple-red foliage

ABOVE *Cardiocrinum giganteum*: slow to grow but spectacular when in bloom

Propagation: Divide plants in the spring after growth has been started; ensure each section has a shoot and some roots

Pests and diseases: Generally free from problems

NAME: *CARDIOCRINUM* (GIANT LILY)
FAMILY: LILIACEAE

Description: These gigantic members of the lily family have a fascination all of their own. *Cardiocrinum giganteum* (AGM), a native of the Himalayas can, in ideal conditions, grow to 8ft (2.4m), producing a magnificent display when its in all its glory. The *Cardiocrinum* is monocarpic, dying after flowering, usually leaving behind one or two offsets that take two or three years to reach flowering size. Planting bulbs of different sizes should ensure that you have some in bloom for most of the year

Popular species and varieties: There is just one species that is generally available – *C. giganteum* (AGM). The stout stem carries long, semi-pendent, trumpet-shaped, fragrant blooms. They are white with a purplish tinge on the inside and a green flush on the outside. The foliage is very different to that of other lilies, in that individual leaves are broad and glossy, and held at the base of the stem. They can be up to 18in (45cm) across, reducing in size up the stem

Where to grow: These very eye-catching plants require a lightly shaded spot in cool, moist, humus-rich soil that has been deeply dug before planting. The spot chosen should not dry out in the summer or become waterlogged. Cardiocrinums die down in the winter with their bulb just below the surface, so ensure that they are not damaged accidentally. In cold districts a mulch of peat or straw will provide some protection

How to grow: Remember that the plants have a considerable spread when in full leaf, so when planted in groups allow 36in (90cm) between each one.

The bulbs should have their tips just below the surface. Planting can be carried out in the autumn or spring

Flowering period: The spectacular flower displays are produced in mid-summer

Maintenance: Despite their height they do not require support. Carefully remove dead foliage after it has died down for the winter

Propagation: Offsets are the best method of propagation in the autumn. Cardiocrinums can be grown from seed, but they can take at least seven years to reach flowering size

Pests and diseases: Generally trouble-free

NAME: *CHIONODOXA* (GLORY OF THE SNOW)
FAMILY: HYACINTHACEAE

Description: A group of dwarf, spring-flowering bulbs. The common name refers to their natural habitat, where they can often be found in bloom, surrounded by melting snow. Chionodoxas seed freely and can, in ideal conditions, soon spread into sizeable colonies. The foliage dies back soon after flowering and seed setting, and as this is during early to mid-spring this does not generally conflict with other plant species coming into growth

Popular species and varieties: One of the best-known members of the family is *C. forbesii* (for many years listed as *C. luciliae*), which has bright blue flowers, each with a white centre. It is a vigorous grower, reaching just 4in (10cm) in height, and it is an ideal subject for naturalizing. There are several named varieties: 'Blue Giant' is as its name indicates; 'Pink Giant', is slightly larger still. Look out for the white form, *C. forbesii* 'Alba'.

Chionodoxa sardensis (AGM) is noted for its true gentian blue flowers with tiny white centres; it also has a dwarf habit reaching just 4in (10cm)

Where to grow: They prefer an open, sunny position, although they will grow successfully in lightly shaded areas. Chionodoxas are good subjects for the rock garden or edge

ABOVE *Chionodoxa forbesii:* one of the best early spring flowers

of a border and also, as mentioned, they are perfectly suited to naturalizing in grass

How to grow: Most good humus-rich, well-drained soils are suitable. Plant *Chinodoxa* in the autumn, 3in (7.5cm) deep, and the same distance apart

Flowering period: Early to mid-spring

Maintenance: Feeding is only required if growing on poor soil

Propagation: Lift and divide when the foliage dies back; replant immediately

Pests and diseases: Generally trouble-free

NAME: *CLIVIA* (KAFFIR LILY)
FAMILY: AMARYLLIDACEAE

Description: A spectacular plant for the heated greenhouse or conservatory. In late winter or early spring it produces stout, flowering stems and clusters of showy blooms over strap-shaped deep green foliage

Popular species and varieties: *Clivia miniata* (AGM) produces bright orange bell-shaped flowers, and has been a great favourite for many years. Now available is the pale yellow *C. m.* var. *citrina* and a number of cultivars, some with cream-striped foliage. In time *C. miniata* will grow into a sizeable clump, carrying a number of long-lasting flower stems each one with up to 20 individual blooms

Where to grow: Select a reasonably light position in the home or conservatory. Avoid direct sunlight, which can scorch the foliage

How to grow: This evergreen plant forms a rhizome. Pot it in a loam-based compost, and keep it in a minimum temperature of 50°F (10°C). Repot only when the plant becomes overcrowded; clivias flower best when they are slightly pot-bound

Flowering period: In some years clivias will start to flower in late winter but it is more usual in the early spring

Maintenance: Remove dead flower heads and stems. Water sparingly in the winter, just enough to avoid the compost from drying out; keep the compost moist from spring through to autumn. An application of a high-potash liquid fertilizer every two weeks in the spring and summer is beneficial. During the summer, plants can be stood outside in a sheltered position

Propagation: Divide plants after flowering, taking care not to damage the rather fragile roots. Clivias may also be raised from seed

Pests and diseases: Mealy bug can attack clivias, producing white, waxy blobs between the leaves. Control with an appropriate systemic insecticide

BELOW *Clivia miniata*: a fine plant for conservatory or greenhouse, flowers best when pot-bound

ABOVE *Colchicum* 'Waterlily': distinctive flower that resembles a waterlily

NAME: *COLCHICUM* (AUTUMN CROCUS)
FAMILY: COLCHICACEAE

Description: Although these very colourful autumn-flowering bulbs are referred to as 'autumn crocus', they are not related to the genuine crocus at all. The name originates from its crocus-like, albeit larger, flower. Suddenly in the autumn their flower buds push through the soil, the foliage follows in the late winter or early spring. Colchicums are large, and have been known to smother small plants. They can look unsightly in a border when dying back, so choose their position with care. All parts of the *Colchicum* are poisonous

Popular species and varieties: One of the best known is the free-flowering *Colchicum autumnale*, which produces a sizeable number of lilac-pink flowers from a single bulb. It is a good plant for naturalizing.

Equally attractive is the white form 'Album'. If you are looking for a real showpiece, then grow 'Alboplenum', a white double producing three to five flowers from each bulb.

'The Giant' always attracts attention with its soft rose-lilac flowers each with a white base. The beautifully framed goblet-shaped flowers stand out well on 10in (25cm) long stalks. Another excellent form is 'Waterlily' (AGM), with purplish-lilac double flowers. In many ways this variety really does resemble a waterlily bloom

Where to grow: Colchicums are good for growing in beds and borders, ideally in small groups. They provide colour when many perennials are past their best. On a rock garden they should be planted only where their spring foliage will not be a distraction. Several forms are good for naturalizing in grass, here again cut the grass but avoid cutting the *Colchicum* foliage until it dies back – remember, they start to flower in the early autumn. These bulbs are happy in a sunny or lightly shaded spot in most humus-rich, well-drained soils

How to grow: Plant the bulbs in late summer in informal groups 4in (10cm) deep and 4–6in (10–15cm) apart

Flowering period: Colchicums are in bloom from late summer to mid-autumn

Maintenance: There is little work required with these plants. Remove dead flowers. The dead foliage will require removal at some stage during early or mid-summer, almost a year after the flowers appeared

Propagation: Lift and divide the clumps in late summer; replant immediately. Colchicums can also be grown from seed, and as in many other cases they can take some time to reach flowering size

Pests and diseases: Generally trouble-free

NAME: *CRINUM* (SWAMP LILY)
FAMILY: AMARYLLIDACEAE

Description: These very attractive plants with their large trumpet-shaped blooms can only be grown successfully outside in a well-sheltered and warm position, ideally at the foot of a south-facing wall

Popular species and varieties: The *Crinum* genus has several species, but just two are

ABOVE *Crinum* x *powellii*: very beautiful pure white blooms

RIGHT *Crocosmia* 'Lady Hamilton': an old favourite

commonly found: *Crinum moorei*, and the hybrid *C. x powellii* (AGM). The latter is best grown in a greenhouse or conservatory.

Crinum moorei is a native of South Africa, and it produces large bulbs. The huge white or pink trumpet blooms are held on stout stems up to 36in (90cm) high, over star-shaped light-green leaves. They dislike disturbance and will build up into sizeable clumps. As mentioned, *C. x powellii* is a tender plant, with flowers varying from pure white to a rich pink

Where to grow: If grown outside only in very sheltered positions, otherwise plant in a frost-free greenhouse, border, or in a pot. Containers can stand outside during the summer, return under glass during the early autumn

How to grow: If outside, plant in the spring 8–12in (20–30cm) deep, and the same distance apart, in good well-drained but moisture-retentive soil. Protect shoots in the spring with peat or fleece.

Crinums grown in containers should be planted in John Innes no. 2 compost with the nose of the bulb just above soil level

Flowering period: Crinums bloom from early summer to early autumn

Maintenance: Remove dead flowers and stems. Crinums planted outside require protection during the winter. Regularly water plants in containers and feed with a balanced liquid fertilizer every two or three weeks after growth starts. Do not disturb plants outside unless overcrowded; those in pots should be repotted every third year

Propagation: Carefully divide clumps in the spring. Offsets can be removed in late winter; pot these individually and grow them on. They should reach flowering size in three years. Crinums can also be grown from seed

Pests and diseases: Generally trouble-free, with the exception of slugs and snails which will attack young foliage and flowers

NAME: *CROCOSMIA* (MONTBRETIA)
FAMILY: IRIDACEAE

Description: In mid-summer few can fail to notice a well-established group of bright red crocosmias in all their glory. Over the years a great many varieties of these popular plants have been introduced to our gardens, making choice difficult

Popular species and varieties: *Crocosmia masoniorum* (AGM) has typical sword-shaped, slightly arching, foliage – typical of most forms.

The red-orange flowers of this species are held on arching stems 5ft (1.5m) in height. Individual blooms comprise long tubes, with well-spread petals and prominent stamens.

When it comes to the named varieties there is certainly plenty of choice, from the fiery-red 'Vulcan' to the very popular 'Lucifer' (AGM), another brilliant red. 'Bressingham Blaze' is another splendid variety with orange-red flowers. 'Emberglow' is similar. There are also a considerable number of yellow-flowered Crocosmia, among them 'Citronella', and the later-flowering 'Solfatare' (AGM), its blooms an attractive apricot-yellow over bronze-flushed foliage

Where to grow: Crocosmias require an open, sunny spot in well-drained soil. They are best in beds and borders and blend in well with many hardy perennials. Heights vary considerably, so check before planting

How to grow: Plant the corms in spring, 3in (7.5cm) deep and around 6in (15cm) apart.

ABOVE *Crocosmia* 'Lucifer': one of the best red varieties

In recent years they have become available as pot-grown plants, and can be planted at any time. In many parts of the garden crocosmias can be left undisturbed for several years

Flowering period: Mid-summer to early autumn, depending on variety

Maintenance: There is little work required, with the exception of cutting off dead flower stems. In the spring a balanced fertilizer can be applied, lightly working it into the soil; take care not to damage new growth. Cut down the dead foliage in autumn. Provide winter protection by covering the crowns of the plants with a mulch of straw, bracken or dry leaves. In very cold districts it is best to lift corms, dry and store them in dry peat, in a frost-free place

Propagation: Lift and divide plants. The best time to do this is immediately after flowering

Pests and diseases: It is unlikely that you will experience any problems with these plants

NAME: *CROCUS*
FAMILY: IRIDACEAE

Description: The *Crocus* is one of the true heralds of spring, following hard on the heels of the snowdrop (*Galanthus*). *Crocus* is among the best known and most popular of all the early blooming bulbs. Most forms are easy to grow, free-flowering and increase well in suitable conditions.

There are over 80 species, many native to Mediterranean countries. Others can be found flowering in high alpine regions as the snow melts which can, depending on season, be as late as mid-summer. Whilst many of the species can be grown in our gardens, those most likely to be found are cultivars

Popular species and varieties: One of the first to flower in late winter and early spring is *Crocus tommasinianus* (AGM); its soft lavender flowers are small and slender. It is happy in a lightly

ABOVE *Crocus tommasinianus* 'Whitwell Purple': an old stager but still one of the best

shaded spot. In ideal conditions it naturalizes freely. Despite flowering early, weak sunshine in mild weather will encourage them to open their flowers wide, making a splendid show particularly when naturalized. They die back quickly after flowering so it is not usually necessary to restrict grass cutting.

There are a number of varieties, some of which are old and familiar forms: one of these is the purplish-blue 'Whitwell Purple'. On the other hand 'Ruby Giant' is, as its name implies, larger, with deep purple flowers produced slightly later.

Crocus in the Chrysanthus group are free flowering. Growing to around 3in (7.5cm) in height, they are at their best from late winter to early spring, depending on conditions. Making a choice from the range available is not easy. Highly recommended are 'Cream Beauty' (AGM), a lovely soft, cream-yellow. Among the best of those with pure white flowers are 'Ard Schenk' and 'Snow Bunting' (AGM). Others to look out for include the popular 'Blue Pearl' (AGM), a lovely delicate blue with a bronze base and silvery blue on the outside of the petals.

ABOVE *Crocus minimus:* masses of small flowers

One with very striking flowers is 'Ladykiller' (AGM), with glistening white slender blooms; its outer petals are a rich purple edged with white. The bright yellow crocus are always popular, including 'E.P. Bowles', with clear yellow flowers, feathered with purple on the outside.

Highly regarded for its fine flowering habit is *C. ancyrensis* 'Golden Bunch', which produces masses of bright orange flowers in early spring. One crocus that became very popular a few years ago is is *Crocus sieberi* 'Tricolor' (AGM). Very distinctive, it is native to southern Greece, and produces lilac blooms, each with a large yellow throat and broad white band.

Dutch crocus are the most widely grown of all. There is a fine range of cultivars available, and most are robust, free-flowering plants with larger blooms than the species. Flowering later than their smaller cousins they also increase rapidly. Often sold as mixed colours, one should not overlook the potential of growing smaller groups of the same variety. Look out for the pure white 'Jeanne d'Arc', the rich purple-violet 'Queen of the Blues', the silvery lilac-blue 'Vanguard', and not forgetting 'Pickwick' with its striking purple striped blooms.

The true autumn crocus should not be confused with colchicums. One of the best spots for these is in an open sunny pocket on the rock garden in well-drained soil. Early autumn is when *Crocus kotschyanus* (AGM) – with its pale lilac yellow-throated blooms – starts to flower. In late autumn the sun-loving saffron crocus (*C. sativus*) appears; its large purple flowers have three deep red stigmas that are the source of the spice saffron

Where to grow: *Crocus* can be grown in many parts of the garden, from naturalization in grass, to an edging for paths and borders, to pockets on the rock garden. Many also make a fine show grown in an alpine or cold greenhouse where their flowers are not spoilt by inclement weather

How to grow: Sunny spots in most well-drained soils are suitable for crocus. Avoid any positions that can become waterlogged. The autumn-flowering crocus should be planted in late summer, and those that flower in the spring should be planted any time from early to mid-autumn.

Always plant in groups for the best effect, with each corm 2in (5cm) deep, and 2–4in (5–10cm) apart. After planting apply a light dressing of bone meal or other well-balanced fertilizer; carefully work this into the soil, taking care not to disturb the bulbs

Flowering period: The 'spring-flowering' crocus actually bloom from late winter to mid-spring, subject to weather conditions. Those that bloom in the autumn do so from early to late autumn, depending on the variety

Maintenance: The grass-like foliage of crocus dies back a few weeks after flowering has finished and should be left to do so naturally, as it is important to build up the corms for the following season. When foliage has turned yellow it can be removed easily

ABOVE *Crocus chrysanthus* 'Ard Schenk': masses of white flowers in early spring

Propagation: Generally, *Crocus* can remain undisturbed for three or four years, when they will require lifting and dividing

Pests and diseases: Birds, particularly sparrows, can destroy the flowers. If this is a problem, protect the blooms with wire netting or a frame covered with fruit netting (unfortunately not very sightly sightly!). Otherwise crocus are trouble-free

ABOVE *Crocus* 'Blue Pearl': lobelia blue with white margin and yellow centre

NAME: *CYCLAMEN*
FAMILY: **PRIMULACEAE**

Description: There are a number of *Cyclamen* species that are splendid garden plants; others are first class subjects for an alpine house. The *Cyclamen persicum* hybrids are well-known indoor plants.

Late winter will often see the charming *C. coum* in all its glory, seemingly quite unaffected by adverse weather. In late summer and early autumn *C. hederifolium* makes a fine show. Both are holders of the Royal Horticultural Society Award of Garden Merit.

The hardy cyclamen are at their best when planted in groups or drifts. In ideal conditions they slowly build up into sizeable colonies where they should remain undisturbed for a number of years

Popular species and varieties: In some years *Cyclamen coum* (AGM) can produce its first flowers in early winter. The pointed buds open to pink or carmine flowers; a white form is also available. Most will have rounded leaves that are dark red on the underside. Some have varying degrees of marbling and silvering on the foliage. These should be found well-protected places, as their foliage can be damaged by severe frosts.

In late summer another great favourite, *C. hederifolium* (AGM), comes into bloom. The first flowers often appear after the ground has become moist following a heavy shower. This cyclamen usually blooms before its foliage commences growth. There are both pink and white forms. A great attraction of the plant is the varied shapes and patterning of the leaves – none are the same, marbling, blotches and silvering all commonplace.

There are many forms of *Cyclamen* suited to the alpine house, including *C. libanoticum* (AGM), which has large clear pink flowers over ivy-shaped leaves in spring. In autumn there is the dainty pink *C. cilicicum* (AGM) and

ABOVE *Cyclamen hederifolium:* flowers in early autumn before foliage appears

ABOVE *Cyclamen coum*: able to withstand inclement weather

C. mirable (AGM), and also *C. graecum*, the pink flowers of which are held well clear of the marbled leaves. They all make a fine show

Where to grow: Both *Cyclamen coum* and *C. hederifolium* are ideal subjects for growing on the rock garden or under trees and shrubs

How to grow: *Cyclamen* grown under glass should be potted in a humus-rich, gritty mixture; top-dress the pot with coarse grit. When watering, take care not to splash leaves or flowers. *Cyclamen coum* and *C. hederifolium* require cool, moist humus-rich, well-drained soil. Plant the tubers with their tops just below the soil. Wherever possible, purchase pot-grown plants, as dry tubers can be difficult to establish and may remain dormant for one or two seasons

Flowering period: Spring, summer or early autumn, depending on the species

Maintenance: Nothing is required to be done outdoors, as *Cyclamen* can be left undisturbed for years. Under glass they will die back after flowering, so withhold water until growth starts again, then increase steadily the amount you give

Propagation: Seed, sown as soon as it is ripe; it takes two or three years for young plants to reach flowering size

Pests and diseases: Vine weevil grubs can cause problems: treat with a suitable pesticide or use natural predators (that can be purchased from specialist suppliers and some garden shops)

NAME: *CYRTANTHUS* (SCARBOROUGH LILY)
FAMILY: **AMARYLLIDACEAE**

Description: Formerly known under the botanical name of *Vallota*, the Scarborough lily is an old favourite. Its correct name now is *Cyrtanthus elatus*, and even its species name has seen changes over the years, having been listed both as *C. purpureus* and *C. speciosus*

Popular species and varieties: This is a tender evergreen bulbous plant originating from South Africa. It has bright green strap-shaped foliage. The 18in (45cm) stout stems have up to eight bright red funnel-shaped blooms, each up to 4in (10cm) across

Where to grow: *Cyrtanthus* should be grown in a pot in a conservatory or greenhouse, or on a sunny windowsill, but not where bright sunlight can scorch the foliage

How to grow: Individual bulbs should be grown in a 5in (12.5cm) pot containing a loam-based compost. Plant the bulb with its tip appearing just above soil level. Several bulbs in a larger container are also very effective.

Cyrtanthus hates disturbance, so leave it in its container for several years; it flowers best when pot-bound. Feed with a good balanced liquid fertilizer monthly during the growing season.

Start into growth in spring, by lightly watering. Reduce water after flowering. Keep plants on the dry side throughout winter, but do not let the compost dry out completely

Flowering period: Early to late summer

Maintenance: Remove dead flower heads and then the later stems as they turn yellow

Propagation: Offsets can be carefully removed, potted up and grown on. They take approximately three years to reach flowering size

Pests and diseases: Problems are seldom encountered with these bulbs

RIGHT **Cyrtanthus elatus**: for many years listed as **Vallota**

NAME: *DAHLIA*
FAMILY: **ASTERACEAE**

Description: There are numerous flower forms of these very popular half-hardy tuberous perennials. These range from the giants whose blooms are 10in (25cm) or more across, to the very neat pompoms with their small, spherical blooms. Colours range from brilliant to subtle, and in most shades except for blue.

Dahlias are excellent for garden decoration and are popular as cut flowers. Each year sees many new varieties making their debut. Having said that, some old stagers are just as popular as ever, and among these there is the ubiquitous 'Bishop of Llandaff' with its dark bronzy leaves and scarlet flowers

Popular species and varieties: Dahlias are divided into a number of types, categorized by the shape of their flowers. One of the most widely grown is the Cactus-type, divided into five further sections, with their fully double blooms and pointed ray florets.

The Decorative group is divided into giant, large, medium, small and miniature. The 'giants' have huge blooms 10in (25cm) or more across. The 'large' have flowers usually between 8–10in (20–25cm) across. The medium and small groups are those often seen in our gardens, the former with blooms of 6–8in (15–20cm), and the latter 4–6in (10–15cm). The miniatures have neat flowers of up to 4in (10cm). The blooms on all of them are fully double without a central disc, the florets are broad and flat.

Other types include the Ball Pompoms, with fully double ball-shaped blooms which can range from 2in (5cm) to 6in (15cm) across

ABOVE *Dahlia* 'Corton Andrea': an attractive example of the Cactus-type

ABOVE *Dahlia* 'Lucky Number': a soft pink decorative variety

depending on type. The Anemone-flowered types, again with double blooms, have their outer florets flat and surrounded by others that are tubular and shorter. There are also other types, less popular but still grown by enthusiasts, including Collerettes and Paeony-flowered types. Finally, do not forget the bedding dahlias that have increased in popularity over the years, neat plants in a wide range of colours and noted for their long periods of flowering.

There are a huge number of *Dahlia* varieties available, with newcomers constantly being added to the already formidable lists. There are too many variety names to mention here, and anyone interested in these plants will find it advisable to obtain one of the specialist catalogues before making a choice

Where to grow: Dahlias are mostly grown in beds or borders. Some of those with a dwarf habit are also suitable for containers. These plants are sun lovers but they should not be planted where they will be subjected to strong winds

How to grow: Before planting, dig over the site and incorporate plenty of well-rotted compost or manure. Dahlias enjoy rich, moist but well-drained soil. Tubers can be potted up

RIGHT *Eranthis hyemalis*: the ever popular winter aconite

or placed in trays or boxes of moist peat-based compost and started into growth in mid-spring in a warm greenhouse.

Alternatively, they can be planted out in late spring when danger of frost has passed. Plant the tubers 4–6in (10–15cm) deep; ensure the neck is pointing upwards. The amount of space allowed between each one depends on variety. For the larger varieties allow distances of 30–36in (75–90cm); for bedding dahlias and small varieties allow 12in (30cm).

It is important to put stakes and labels in at planting time to avoid any possible damage later. Tie as required throughout the season. When they are growing well pinch out the leading shoots; this will result in a bushier plant. Disbud regularly (leaving the top bud and carefully pinching the two smaller buds below); this ensures bigger and better (but slightly fewer) blooms. Dead-head plants on a regular basis

Flowering period: Mid-summer to early autumn

Maintenance: Dahlias are heavy feeders, and once flowering has commenced it is important to feed plants with a well-balanced liquid fertilizer every 14 days. Water well in hot, dry conditions during the growing season. A mulch of well-rotted compost is advisable as this will help to retain moisture.

The first frost of autumn will blacken the foliage; this is the time to cut plants down to within a few inches of ground level. Carefully lift the plants and dry off, clean and store them for the winter in dry peat in a frost-free place. Inspect the tubers periodically for signs of disease or shrivelling. Any damaged parts can be cut out and the wound dusted with sulphur-based fungicide. Placing shrivelled tubers in water and keeping them there overnight will plump them up; dry off well before returning them to the store

Propagation: The usual method of increasing stock is by division in mid-spring. Ensure that an undamaged 'eye' (or growth bud) remains on each portion. Dust any cut parts with sulphur powder, which will protect them from fungus attack. If necessary, pot up until either the ground is ready or danger of frost has passed.

Cuttings can be taken from tubers that have already started into growth. Take these when around 3in (7.5cm) in length; remove the lower set of leaves and dip the base of the cutting in rooting compound. Insert it into an equal mixture of peat and sand. When well

rooted, pot up the cuttings individually and grow them on until they are ready to plant out

Pests and diseases: Keep a careful check for aphids, as these can transmit virus diseases. Spray with a suitable insecticide as soon as the pests are seen. Caterpillars, capsid bugs and earwigs can all be controlled by spraying with a suitable insecticide.

Virus diseases can cause stunting, distorting and yellowing of foliage: with viruses there is no cure, so lift and destroy any plants affected

NAME: *ERANTHIS* (WINTER ACONITE)
FAMILY: RANUNCULACEAE

Description: The appearance of aconites in late winter, even when melting snow is still on the ground, is a true reminder that spring in not too far away. These distinctive, glossy, cup-shaped flowers with their ruff of green deeply toothed leaves are truly a cheerful sight after the long dreary days of winter

Popular species and varieties: The true winter aconite is *Eranthis hyemalis* (AGM), and it is a good, low-growing companion for snowdrops and hellebores. In ideal conditions it will seed itself, in time forming a carpet of buttercup-yellow blooms in late winter. *Eranthis cilicica* flowers in late winter, it has finely divided bronze foliage and large deep golden-yellow flowers. The most impressive of all is the vigorous 'Guinea Gold' (AGM), a variety of *E. x tubergenii* with large golden-yellow showy flowers

Where to grow: Aconites will grow successfully in any open, sunny, or lightly shaded spot, in moisture-retentive but free-draining humus-rich soil

How to grow: Aconites are often sold as dry tubers, and in the autumn these can be very dry and difficult to start into growth. Soaking overnight or placing in damp peat can help. Alternatively, they can be purchased as growing plants in the spring.

Plant tubers at a depth of 1–2in (2.5–5cm), and around 4in (10cm) apart. Autumn is the best time to plant, or in spring as 'growing plants', the ideal time to ensure they settle down quickly.

Aconites require moist conditions in the spring, especially when growing under trees. In conditions well suited to them they can become invasive, but are unlikely to cause problems as they die back fairly quickly after flowering

Flowering period: Mid- to late winter

Maintenance: Within several weeks after flowering has finished the foliage turns yellow. Keep an eye open for ripening seed that can be scattered in other places around the garden

Propagation: This is usually by careful division of crowded tubers; replant immediately. Alternatively, in the case of species aconites, grow from seed

Pests and diseases: Generally trouble-free

NAME: *ERYTHRONIUM* (DOG'S TOOTH VIOLET) FAMILY: LILIACEAE

Description: Many of these very desirable plants are native to the United States, while *Erythronium dens-canis* (AGM) can be found in Central Europe and parts of Asia. The rather curious common name originates from the shape of the fleshy pointed bulb that loosely resembles a dog's tooth. Erythroniums are woodland plants and are suitable for growing under deciduous trees or on a lightly shaded rock garden

Popular species and varieties: The well-known and easily grown *E. dens-canis* is a plant that is often to be seen in cottage gardens. The pink-purple flowers are held over foliage mottled green and brown. There are a number of named cultivars, among them 'Rose Queen' with deep pink blooms, and 'White Splendour', white.

Another particularly attractive member of the family is *E. californicum* (AGM), which has mid-green foliage that is lightly mottled silvery green. The cream-white flowers with their reflexed petals are held on stems 8in (20cm) high. Look out for the exquisite pure white 'White Beauty' (AGM). Its blooms have soft yellow anthers that contrast well against chocolate brown-centred leaves.

Also known by the common name of American trout lily, *Erythronium revolution* (AGM) is another good choice; its pink flowers on strong 12in (30cm) high stems are held well clear of the brown-purple mottled foliage.

One of the most popular of all the erythroniums is a hybrid: 'Pagoda' (AGM). This is a vigorous plant, which in ideal conditions will naturalize itself. The larger flowers are pendent yellow, and four or five may be carried on a single 12in (30cm) stem

Where to grow: Select a place that is lightly shaded. This can be in a border, on the rock garden or under deciduous trees

ABOVE *Erythronium* 'Kondo': one of the best yellow-flowered varieties

ABOVE *Erythroniums* enjoy cool moist lightly shaded spots

How to grow: Erythroniums require cool, moist humus-rich conditions. Avoid any places that are badly drained. Plant the tubers in late summer or early autumn in groups 4–6in (10–15cm) deep, and around 6in (15cm) apart. Purchase tubers early in the season and ensure they do not dry out. Plant them as soon as possible. Tubers that have been allowed to become too dry in storage can be difficult to start into growth

Flowering period: Early to mid-spring

Maintenance: Keep the soil moist in any hot, dry spells. The foliage will die down fairly quickly after flowering has finished. Remove dead foliage. It is not necessary to feed the plants. In late winter a top dressing of well-rotted leaf mould or compost is beneficial. Erythroniums hate disturbance

Propagation: In late summer lift and carefully divide; replant immediately. They can also be grown from seed, but the resulting plants may be variable

Pests and diseases: These are ideal garden subjects, as they are generally trouble-free

NAME: *EUCOMIS* (PINEAPPLE LILY)
FAMILY: HYACINTHACEAE

Description: Many of the most attractive bulbous plants originate from South Africa. One such is the pineapple lily, *Eucomis*, taking its common name from its flower spike, which resembles that of a pineapple with its top crown of tufted leaves

Popular species and varieties: The species most often encountered is *Eucomis bicolor*,

ABOVE *Eucomis comosa*: grow in a sheltered spot or a tub

which grows to around 30in (75cm) in height, with its green and purple-edged flower spike about 12in (30cm) in length. The stout stem is also heavily blotched with purple. There is also a white form listed as 'Alba'. Mid-summer onwards is when *E. autumnalis* produces its flowering spikes of pure white followed by attractive seed heads

Where to grow: *Eucomis* is an excellent plant for a container. It can be grown outdoors in mild districts, in a very sheltered position – at the base of a sunny wall is ideal

How to grow: In containers, plant the bulbs 2–4in (5–10cm) deep using John Innes no. 2 or soil-less compost. Outdoors, grow them in well-drained, humus-rich soil

Flowering period: Mid- to late summer

Maintenance: Container-grown plants should be taken inside to a frost-free place for the winter. Outdoors they can be left *in situ* in mild, very sheltered positions. Apply a protective mulch of peat or bracken. Alternatively, lift and store in dry peat for the winter in a frost-free place. Keep soil or compost moist during the growing season. Apply periodic applications of a good liquid general fertilizer after growth commences until the foliage starts to turn yellow

Propagation: Divide the clumps in autumn

Pests and diseases: Usually no problems occur, but be aware of slugs and snails that often attack the foliage; protect as necessary

NAME: *FREESIA*
FAMILY: **IRIDACEAE**

Description: Most of the freesias grown today are hybrids that are available in a wide range of colours, from red, blue, mauve and pink to yellow and white. These hybrids grow to around 18in (45cm) in height, taller than the species. Freesias are usually noted for their strong perfume as well as their

RIGHT *Freesia* 'Oberon': freesias are widely grown for indoor decoration

78

RIGHT *Fritillaria imperialis*: the stately crown imperial

colourful flowers, but it should be known that some do not have any scent at all.

The majority of freesias are grown under glass. Many bulb merchants now supply outdoor freesias; these have been 'prepared', and can be planted outside in a warm, sheltered position

Popular species and varieties: Freesias are usually sold in mixtures, especially those for outside. It is also possible to purchase some individual varieties, among them 'Elegance' and 'Miranda' both with white blooms. 'Beethoven' is a rich, light creamy yellow. Especially attractive are 'Yellow River' and 'Wintergold', and the lovely red forms 'Escapade' and 'Oberon'. The double, pale-purple 'Romany' should not be overlooked

Where to grow: Those grown indoors require a cool greenhouse or conservatory at a maximum winter temperature of 50°F (10°C). Take them indoors when the buds are beginning to show some colour. After flowering take them back to the greenhouse; keep in growth, and when the foliage dies back dry them off for the summer. If growing them outdoors, select a sheltered, sunny position

How to grow: During autumn plant six corms 2in (5cm) deep in a 5in (12.5cm) pot. Use John Innes no. 2 or soil-less compost. While the shoots and leaves are developing, ensure that the compost is always moist, but not too wet. New growth should be visible in late autumn.

The outdoor freesias must be grown in a well-drained sandy soil; plant the corms 2in (5cm) deep in groups

Flowering period: Indoors – early to late winter; outdoors – mid-summer onwards

Maintenance: Apply a high-potash liquid fertilizer every 14 days through the growing season. When the foliage has died back lift the corms and dry them off; store them in an airy frost-free place over winter

Propagation: When lifting corms remove offsets and grow them on in the same way. Feed them and they will often flower the following year

Pests and diseases: Aphids should be controlled immediately they are seen, as they can transmit virus diseases. Fungal disease can attack when grown under glass

NAME: *FRITILLARIA* (CROWN IMPERIAL, SNAKE'S HEAD FRITILLARY)
FAMILY: LILIACEAE

Description: Unquestionably the most spectacular member of this family is *Fritillaria imperialis*, which is often referred to by its common name of crown imperial. These very impressive plants have a rather unpleasant fox-like scent, but this should in no way deter anyone from growing them. A large group in all their glory is a magnificent sight, with their stout stems and sizeable bell-shaped blooms. It is recorded as having been grown in British gardens as early as 1575

Popular species and varieties: *Fritillaria imperialis* is a native of the Himalayas and grows to around 36in (90cm) in height. The narrow, glossy leaves are produced in whorls

81

ABOVE *Fritillaria 'Maxima Lutea'*: the lovely yellow form is equally popular

along the stem with the rich red flowers in a terminal cluster. There are several named varieties, including 'Maxima Lutea' (AGM) with golden-yellow flowers, and 'The Premier', a soft tangerine-orange

One species that has in recent years become much more readily available is *F. persica*, with 'Adiyaman' (AGM) noted for its dark, plum-purple, bell-shaped flowers along most of its 24in (60cm) stem. This is a vigorous plant with plain green foliage

Few can fail to admire the chequered flowers of the snake's head fritillary, *F. meleagris* (AGM). This is a native of central and eastern Europe and also Great Britain. The bell-shaped pendant flowers are held in pairs on wiry 8in (20cm) stems. Each individual bloom has purple chequered markings. One should not overlook the lovely pure white 'Aphrodite'.

There are numerous other species, some easy to grow, while others require growing in an alpine house. In recent years *F. michailovskyi*

(AGM) has become very popular due to its eye-catching purple-brown, yellow-edged, bell-shaped flowers on 8in (20cm) stems

Where to grow: Fritillarias generally require a lightly shaded place in the garden, but *F. imperialis* can be particularly successful in full sun. This, and *F. persica*, are ideal subjects for beds or borders. The lovely *F. meleagris* can also be grown at the front of a border but is best in a pocket on the rock garden; it can also be naturalized in grass

How to grow: Fritillarias need a good humus-rich, moist but not waterlogged soil. They do not like being disturbed once established. *F. imperialis* should be planted in the autumn at a depth of 8in (20cm); *F. persica* should be set 6in (15cm) deep. Both should be spaced 8–12in (20–30cm) apart. The much smaller *F. meleagris* should be planted 2in (5cm) deep, and the same distance apart.

The large bulbs of the crown imperial are hollow. Lay each bulb on its side, on a bed of sand, so that water cannot collect in the hollow and cause it to rot. Once planted they start to produce roots early; if these roots are present when you first buy the bulbs, take care not to damage them when transporting or planting. Leave the plants undisturbed for four years

Flowering period: Early to mid-spring

Maintenance: Apply a high-potash feed to the tallest varieties as soon as growth starts in the spring. Water the plants during hot, dry spells. Staking is not required, even with the tallest forms. When the plants have died back in the autumn remove dead foliage

Propagation: Divide any crowded clumps in the summer, and replant immediately. Seed is another method of increasing stock of many species. It is a lengthy business, taking four to six years before reaching flowering size

Pests and diseases: Generally trouble-free

ABOVE *Fritillaria persica* 'Adiyaman': masses of dark plum purple bell-shaped flowers

ABOVE *Fritillaria meleagris*: the well-known 'Snake's Head Fritillary'

NAME: *GALANTHUS* (SNOWDROP)
FAMILY: **AMARYLLIDACEAE**

Description: The snowdrop is unquestionably one of the best loved of all our early bulbs, flowering in late winter, and seemingly able to withstand all that the weather can throw at them. These bulbous plants, with their nodding white flowers, let us know that spring is not too far away. Such is the interest in *Galanthus* that they have a large following, with enthusiasts studying flower shape and the most minute markings of these very attractive plants. Gardens where snowdrops exist in large drifts attract visitors from far and wide

Popular species and varieties: The best known is the common snowdrop, *Galanthus nivalis* (AGM), a native of Europe including parts of Great Britain. Many plants growing in the wild have become naturalized from gardens. It grows from 4–8in (10–20cm) high, and produces its finest show in humus-rich soil and partial shade. The glaucous leaves are flat and strap shaped; the white flowers have green markings on the inner petals. There is also a double form, 'Flore Pleno' (AGM), and numerous named varieties, among them 'Viridapicis', with a green spot on both the inner and outer petals. Another double is 'Lady Elphinstone' with yellow markings.

A great favourite is *G. elwesii* (AGM), widely known as the giant snowdrop. It has broad, greyish foliage and large flowers held on 10in (25cm) stems. The blooms have three long petals, and three shorter ones with bright green markings. It is often into early spring

ABOVE *Galanthus elwesii*: noted for its large flowers

when *G. ikariae* flowers; the foliage is broad and a bright glossy green. This is a distinctive variety with long outer petals, the shorter inner ones have typical green markings.

There are numerous hybrids including 'Magnet' (AGM) with long slender pedicels, the rather heavy flowers move in the slightest breeze. One of the finest snowdrops is 'S. Arnott' (AGM), which has rounded, bell-shaped, fragrant flowers on 8in (20cm) stems. 'Straffan' is an old favourite with large blooms on 6in (15cm) high stems

Where to grow: Partial shade, in a position where the bulbs will not be subjected to baking in summer, such as under deciduous trees or shrubs, is ideal

How to grow: Snowdrops will grow happily in most cool, humus-rich soils, but will perform even better in heavy loam, neutral to alkaline soils. Dry bulbs can be difficult to establish, so it is best to buy snowdrops as growing plants, known as 'in the green' (available from specialists); these will grow away quickly. Bulbs should be planted in the autumn, 3–4in (7.5–10cm) deep, and about the same distance apart

Flowering period: Mid- to late winter, depending on variety

Maintenance: Mulching in the autumn, with well-rotted compost, is beneficial

Propagation: Lift and divide as soon as flowering has finished; replant immediately, taking care not to damage the roots. It is important that they are replanted at the same depth. Seed can be scattered at random if you wish them to naturalize, but it will take many years for them to reach flowering size

Pests and diseases: Stem and bulb eelworm cause discoloration, rotting and ultimately the loss of the plant

NAME: *GALTONIA* (SUMMER HYACINTH, SPIRE LILY)
FAMILY: **HYACINTHACEAE**

Description: These tall spikes of white, bell-shaped flowers produced from mid-summer onwards are a welcome addition to any border. This member of the *Hyacinth* family is slightly scented, and like so many of our favourite bulbous plants, it is a native plant of South Africa

Popular species and varieties: There are four species of *Galtonia* but only one is usually seen in our gardens, *G. candicans*. It is widely regarded as being the hardiest.

The tall flowering spikes of this plant grow to 4ft (1.2m) and carry ten or more white flowers on a short stalk. Each individual bloom has pale green markings on the base and at the tip of the petals. The leaves are glossy, narrow and semi-erect

Where to grow: Galtonias are best suited to borders, or among shrubs. Choose an open, sunny spot, and plant in groups of three or five

How to grow: Plant the round bulbs during spring, at a depth of 6in (15cm), and the same distance apart, in a good, well-drained soil

Flowering period: Mid- to late summer

Maintenance: Galtonias produce strong stems, and support is not required. Leave them undisturbed, and in the autumn tidy away dead foliage and flower stems

Propagation: These plants are slow to produce offsets. During autumn separate them carefully from the parent bulb, and replant them immediately. In most seasons seed is produced; this can be saved and sown in the spring, but this is a long process taking four or five years for the bulbs to reach flowering size

Pests and diseases: *Galtonia* bulbs can sometimes be attacked by the fungal disease grey mould (botrytis)

RIGHT Galtonias: often referred to as summer hyacinths

NAME: *GLADIOLUS* (SWORD LILY)
FAMILY: **IRIDACEAE**

Description: It may come as a surprise to many that there are around 300 species of *Gladiolus*, many originating from South Africa. It is the modern garden hybrids in a wide spectrum of colours that are most widely grown today. The *Gladiolus* is not hardy, so lifting the corms in the autumn and replanting in the spring is essential

Popular species and varieties: *Gladiolus communis* subsp. *byzantinus* (AGM) is a plant from Mediterranean regions. In many mild districts it can be left in the ground undisturbed. The flower spike is 24in (60cm) high, with loosely arranged wine-red florets.

The large-flowered hybrids come in a wide range of colours and there are countless varieties available. Among them are: 'Advance', a glowing red, 'Jacksonville', a deep yellow with a red throat, and 'Mysterious', a ruffled rose-pink with white a centre. There are many others from which to choose.

Butterfly gladiolus are smaller flowered, growing up to 36in (90cm), and are widely used in floral arrangements. Many of the florets are ruffled or frilled. 'Anglia' is an eye-catching yellow with a red mark, 'Farandole' is a rich vermilion red, and 'Yellow Gem' a striking mimosa-yellow.

The flowers of *Primulinus gladiolus* are funnel shaped; the upper petal forms a hood, and the florets are not so densely packed on the stem. 'Columbine' is a good carmine-red, 'Anitra' is a rich red, and the lovely 'Lady Godiva' is white

Where to grow: Gladioli are not universally popular garden plants, many gardeners preferring to grow them instead in rows in the kitchen garden, or on a spare piece of ground, to provide cut flowers for indoors.

LEFT *Gladiolus*: the small-flowered gladioli are very popular

It can be difficult to find a suitable place to grow them, and they do require staking

How to grow: In a sunny place in good, humus-rich, well-drained soil. Plant in spring 3–4in (7.5–10cm) deep, and 6in (15cm) apart. Stagger planting between early and late spring to give a succession of blooms

Flowering period: Summer

Maintenance: On most soils feeding is not required; the exception is poor soil, in which case a balanced fertilizer should be applied before planting. Staking is usually needed for the large-flowered types. In hot, dry conditions it is important to water the plants well. As the foliage starts to turn yellow lift the corms; cut the foliage and stalks off near the corm, and dry the corm in a warm, airy place for several weeks. Then clean the corm, remove old roots, outer skin and old shrivelled corm at the base. They can then be stored over winter in a dry, frost-free place

Propagation: Remove the small cormlets from the parent bulb, store separately as above. Grow these on for the next year; during the second year most should have reached flowering size

Pests and diseases: Aphids should, if seen, be dealt with promptly. Thrips can also be a problem. Stored corms can be attacked by a 'corm rot', for which there is no cure. Several fungal diseases can attack growing plants

NAME: *GLORIOSA* (GLORY LILY)
FAMILY: **COLCHICACEAE**

Description: The *Gloriosa* is a very attractive and spectacular tuberous-rooted climbing plant that requires greenhouse or conservatory conditions. It has a long flowering period and should be positioned where its unusual lily-like flowers can be admired to the full

Popular species and varieties: The glory lily usually listed as *Gloriosa rothschildiana*, or now more correctly *Gloriosa superba* 'Rothschildiana', grows up to 6ft (1.8m).

ABOVE *Gloriosa rothschildiana:* a very impressive climbing plant

The oval leaves have tendrils at their tips by which the plant supports itself. Trellis or twigs are also required for support. The blooms are produced singly from upper leaf axils. There is a certain amount of variation among the flowers, with crimson and yellow and wavy-edged reflexing petals the form most often seen.

There is also the plain yellow 'Lutea'

Where to grow: Bright conditions are required, but if grown in a greenhouse or conservatory supply a little shade

How to grow: Gloriosas produce long finger-like tubers that should be handled carefully, especially the tips. In late winter or early spring select an 8in (20cm) pot and plant the tuber at a depth of around 6in (15cm), in John Innes no. 2 or soil-less compost. Water sparingly; growth will commence fairly quickly, when the amount given can be increased. Avoid over-watering. During the growing season apply high-potash liquid fertilizer every two weeks

Flowering period: Mid- to late summer

Maintenance: When flowering has finished, withhold water and allow the pot to dry out for winter storage. Store in a frost-free place at a temperature of 50°F (10°C) until restarting into growth in the spring. Poor drainage or over-watering can result in the tubers rotting

Propagation: In early spring carefully divide the tubers, making sure each piece has a growing point. Pot these up and grow on

Pests and diseases: No problems are usually experienced. Beware of slugs that can damage the tubers

NAME: *HEDYCHIUM* (GINGER LILY)
FAMILY: *ZINGERBERACEAE*

Description: These are generally plants for the greenhouse or conservatory, although *Hedychium gardnerianum* (AGM) can be grown successfully in the border during the summer months. These plants should survive the winter outdoors in very mild districts, if in a sheltered spot

ABOVE *Hedychium gardnerianum:* fragrant flowers in late summer

91

Popular species and varieties: Although there are a number of species, the one that is normally seen in our gardens is the Kahili ginger, *H. gardnerianum*, a native of India. This is a vigorous plant growing up to 5ft (1.5m) in height, and with a spread of 4ft (1.2m) or more. The mid-green leaves are lance shaped. In mid-summer the heads of the distinctive yellow flowers with their prominent brilliant red stamens start to appear, and then go on for several weeks.

H. coccineum (AGM) is another native of India. This does not grow as tall, reaching 4ft (1.2m). The flowers are red and are carried in terminal clusters

Where to grow: Unless you live in very mild districts, hedychiums are best regarded as pot or container subjects, and can be stood outdoors on a patio in summer. They can also be planted in the border for the summer months

How to grow: These are rhizome-forming plants. In pots or containers use John Innes no. 3 compost. If planting out, a humus-rich, well-drained soil is required. Plants should be fed in the summer every two weeks, with a good liquid general fertilizer

Flowering period: Flowering commences in mid-summer and carries on into early autumn

Maintenance: Remove dead flower heads. Container-grown plants should be covered before the first sharp autumn frosts. Cut down the foliage when it has died back. Keep the plants in their containers over winter and repot every second year. Those grown outside for the summer should be cut down when the foliage has died back. Lift the rhizomes carefully and store in dry peat in a frost-free, airy place until the following spring

Propagation: Carefully divide the rhizomes during spring

Pests and diseases: Usually trouble-free

NAME: *HIPPEASTRUM*
FAMILY: **AMARYLLIDACEAE**

Description: These flamboyant bulbous plants are often incorrectly referred to as *Amaryllis*. Their very spectacular flowers produced in the winter months make them one of the most popular houseplants and, as a result, they are available from many sources. Each bulb produces between two and six huge trumpet-shaped flowers on a thick stem of around 18in (45cm) high. Most come in various shades of red or pink; some have delicate or bold shading

Popular species and varieties: There are a whole host of named varieties. Among those to look out for are 'Red Peacock' – a brilliant scarlet, and the ever-popular 'Apple Blossom' – pale pink or white flowers with a green centre. Others include 'Rilona', salmon pink, 'Star of Holland', bright red flowers with a distinctive band along the centre of each petal, and the spectacular 'Mont Blanc', pure white

Where to grow: These are splendid subjects for the home, conservatory or heated greenhouse. They require bright light and many are grown in a window, where they receive maximum light

How to grow: The large bulbs should be planted in John Innes no. 2 or a good soil-less compost, in a pot that is around 1in (2.5cm) larger than the circumference of the bulb. Place enough compost in the pot so that the bulb rests on it and when topped up it leaves the upper half of the bulb uncovered. If planted in late summer or early autumn they should flower from mid-winter. After planting, give just enough water to keep the compost from drying out until growth starts – often the flower bud is first to appear – from then on water more freely. After growth has started apply a high-potash liquid fertilizer every seven to ten days. Continue to water and feed throughout the flowering period and until the foliage starts to turn yellow; then withhold watering completely, and allow the compost to dry out

ABOVE *Hippeastrum* 'Star of Holland': often referred to as *Amarylis*

Flowering period: Flower buds take about seven to ten weeks to start into growth from planting. Most flower from mid-winter to early spring

Maintenance: Repot bulbs in the autumn and start them into growth

Propagation: Offsets can be removed in the autumn and grown on

Pests and diseases: Mealy bugs can attack bulbs and foliage; treat with a suitable systemic insecticide as soon as symptoms are seen

93

NAME: *HYACINTHOIDES* (BLUEBELL)
FAMILY: *HYACINTHACEAE*

The Spanish bluebell, *Hyacinthoides hispanica*, was for many years listed as *Scilla campanulata*. It is a splendid plant for growing in groups in the border – robust and free flowering with forms available in blue, pink and white. Large bell-shaped blooms are carried on stems 12in (30cm) high from mid- to late spring. They are frequently sold in colour mixtures, but in my opinion look far better in groups of the same colour. It is also excellent for naturalizing in woodlands or lightly shaded sites

Popular species and varieties: *Hyacinthoides hispanica* is a lovely rich blue; 'Queen of the Pinks' is, as its name indicates, a delicate rose-pink. Among those with snow white flowers is 'White City'.

The English bluebell, *H. non-scripta*, is smaller. It has arching stems and purple-blue flowers that are tubular and are held on one side. It is widely available commercially, and so it is neither sensible, nor correct, to collect it from its wild habitats: the fear of many conservationists is that the natural and wild plantings of these plants are fast disappearing, and because of this raiders of wild plants are regularly prosecuted in the UK

Where to grow: *Hyacinthoides hispanica* looks good in groups among deciduous shrubs, adding bold splashes of colour among the new foliage of spring. There are many other places around the garden where it has much to offer, and can even be grown to great effect in a container. *Hyacinthoides non-scripta* is best confined to woodland areas. It can be invasive and is best left to naturalize under deciduous trees where it will provide a wonderful sight in late spring

LEFT *Hyacinthoides hispanica*: the pink form of Spanish bluebell

RIGHT *Hyacinthoides hispanica*: for years listed as *Scilla campanulata*

How to grow: Plant the bulbs in late summer or early autumn, 2in (5cm) deep and about 3–4in (7.5–10cm) apart. Regular feeding is not required; a light sprinkling of bone meal gently worked into the soil in early spring is beneficial

Flowering period: Mid- to late spring

Maintenance: Unless self-seeding is required, remove dead flowers before seed heads ripen. Remove dead foliage only after it has died back. Leave plants undisturbed for two or three years, only lift and divide when they become overcrowded

Propagation: Lift and divide in late summer; replant immediately

Pests and diseases: Generally trouble-free

ABOVE *Hyacinth* 'Carnegie': fragrant heads of pure white flowers

NAME: *HYACINTHUS* (HYACINTH)
FAMILY: **HYACINTHACEAE**

Description: Unsurpassed for their delightful fragrance, it is hardly surprising that these colourful subjects are among the most popular of all spring-flowering bulbs. They provide a magnificent show massed in beds, or in small groups in the front of a border. The best plantings comprise just one colour; mixed plantings are seldom effective as different varieties are at their best at slightly different times.

Hyacinths produce their finest blooms in the first year, with densely massed heads of small bell-shaped flowers. In subsequent years, while every bit as attractive, the blooms are looser and have fewer flowers.

The majority of hyacinths, often referred to as the Dutch hybrids, have been developed from *Hyacinthus orientalis*. One has only to look through the pages of a specialist bulb supplier's catalogue, or among the displays in late spring, to appreciate the wide colour range available

Popular species and varieties: Many of the older varieties remain equally as popular today. Among the most well-known are the large-flowering, mid-blue 'Delft Blue' (AGM), one of the best yellows, 'City of Haarlem' (AGM), and not forgetting the white 'L'Innocence' (AGM).

Others to look out for include the rosy red 'Amsterdam', and two very different blue varieties: 'Blue Giant', a pale sky blue, and 'Blue Jacket' (AGM), with its striking dark blue heads. One that never fails to attract attention is 'Gipsy Queen' (AGM), a lovely shade of yellow flushed with apricot. Do not miss the smaller-flowered 'Woodstock', purple, or 'Carnegie', pure white.

The Cynthella hybrids are smaller, with blooms held on 6in (15cm) stems, and are normally sold in colour mixtures

ABOVE *Hyacinth* 'Gipsy Queen': best described as Chinese yellow

ABOVE *Hyacinth* 'Delft Blue': an old stager but still among the best

RIGHT *Hymenocallis* x *festalis*: pure white flowers with long, narrow segments

Where to grow: Hyacinths will grow well in a sunny or lightly shaded spot in humus-rich, well-drained soil. Avoid dense shade or wet soils that could cause the bulbs to rot. Hyacinths are also very successful when grown in patio containers, window boxes and in pots in a cold greenhouse

How to grow: Always plant in groups of the same variety with the exception of the miniatures (Cynthella). Plant 6in (15cm) deep and 6–8in (15–20cm) apart. A sprinkling of balanced general fertilizer or bone meal lightly worked in after flowering is beneficial. In hot, dry weather hyacinths in containers may require watering. Bulbs that have been grown for indoor decoration should be planted in the garden as soon as possible after flowering has finished

Flowering period: Late winter and early spring

Maintenance: Cut off dead flower heads and leave the foliage to die back naturally before removing it. Hyacinths can cause a reaction to some people with sensitive skin – if necessary wear gloves when handling

Propagation: By division in early autumn; offsets will take some time to reach flowering size

Pests and diseases: Grey bulb rot can destroy bulbs and cause stunted foliage; lift and destroy any affected bulbs. Note that disease can remain in the soil and affect other bulbs in the following year. Hyacinths can also fall victim to fungal disease when in storage

NAME: *HYMENOCALLIS* (SPIDER LILY, PERUVIAN DAFFODIL)
FAMILY: AMARYLLIDACEAE

Description: Spider lilies are best grown in a conservatory or greenhouse. Only in very sheltered positions and in mild climates can they be grown outdoors. They can still occasionally be found referred to by their old name of *Ismene*.

Recent years have seen the plants become more widely available from specialist bulb suppliers and they can also be found on sale at some of the larger garden centres

Popular species and varieties: The best known is *Hymenocallis* x *festalis* with its large, scented white flowers up to 6in (15cm) across. It is noted for its free-flowering habit. The strap-like leaves are mid-green. Each bloom has a trumpet-shaped central cup with long narrow petal-like segments surrounding it. Also widely available

is the primrose-yellow 'Sulphur Queen', with four to six flowers on each strong stem. The throat is light yellow with green stripes

Where to grow: In pots and containers under glass. Or outside in borders, but only in the most sheltered spots in very mild areas

How to grow: Plant the bulbs in early spring with the neck just below the surface. Plant one large bulb per 6in (15cm) pot or, for a very dramatic show, plant three in a larger container. Use a light, open compost. Water sparingly until growth starts, and as the buds form apply a high-potash liquid feed every two weeks, and continue this during the summer. When foliage starts to die back withhold water and store the pots in a frost-free place

Flowering period: Late spring and early summer

Maintenance: Lift any bulbs grown outside after they have died down and store in dry peat in a frost-free airy place until spring

Propagation: Remove any offsets at repotting time and grow these on

Pests and diseases: No problems are normally encountered with these bulbs

ABOVE *Ipheion* 'Rolf Fielder': best grown in an alpine house

NAME: *IPHEION* (SPRING STARFLOWER)
FAMILY: **ALLIACEAE**

Description: These easily grown bulbous plants are ideal for edging paths, sunny pockets on the rock garden and are very useful for naturalizing among other spring–flowering bulbs. They have an onion smell when crushed, which is hardly surprising considering they are in the onion family

Popular species and varieties: *Ipheion uniflorum* produces a considerable number of narrow grey-green leaves in late winter. The slightly fragrant, pale blue star-shaped flowers are carried on 6in (15cm) stems in early spring. Several varieties are available: 'Wisley Blue', violet-blue flowers in late spring; 'Froyle Mill' (AGM), a slightly different shade and 'Album', pure white.

'Rolf Fiedler' (AGM), is a lovely clear blue, and is best grown in an alpine house or sunny, sheltered spot

Where to grow: Ipheions are sun lovers, ideal as an edging to paths, clumps at the front of a border, or naturalized in grass under deciduous trees

How to grow: Plant in late summer or early autumn, 2in (5cm) deep and the same distance apart. Water in hot, dry spells. When flowering has finished sprinkle a light dressing of a good general fertilizer and work it carefully into the soil

Flowering period: Depending on variety, early spring to early summer

Maintenance: These are not demanding plants at all. Remove dead heads and leaves. Clumps can become overcrowded, which results in fewer flowers being produced. If this happens lift and divide

Propagation: By division of the bulbs in autumn; replant immediately

Pests and diseases: Generally no problems

BELOW *Ipheion uniflorum*: masses of pale blue flowers; bulbs can be naturalized

NAME: *IRIS*
FAMILY: **IRIDACEAE**

There are two main types of iris – those grown from rhizomes, and others grown from bulbs. Among the former are the flamboyant bearded iris that provide colour in early summer; the bulbous type include the winter-flowering Reticulata group and the elegant summer-flowering Junos.

RHIZOMATOUS IRIS

Description: Many gardeners will be familiar with the tall bearded irises with their stiff, sword-shaped foliage. Mostly we grow the hybrids, of which there are many, with newcomers continually being added to the already formidable lists. Such is the range of colours and combinations that it is best to study an iris specialist's catalogue, or look for them in springtime at a garden centre

Popular species and varieties: The tall bearded types include *Iris germanica* (AGM), often referred to as purple flag, or London flag. In late spring and early summer they produce scented blooms with rich purple falls and a white beard; the standards are of light purple. It grows to 24–36in (60–90cm), depending on the variety.

The dwarf bearded irises are excellent for the front of a border or sunny pocket on the rock garden. Their heights range from 4–12in (10–30cm). They are fully hardy and are again available in a wide range of colours.

ABOVE *Iris* 'Harmony': grow in groups – flowers early

ABOVE *Iris* 'Katherine Hodgkin': outstanding flowers in early summer

There are several irises suitable for water and bog gardens. The best known is the yellow flag, *I. pseudacorus* (AGM). This is one for the edge of a large pond or lake, growing to 4ft (1.2m) it is too large for smaller gardens. It will grow happily in shallow water.

The Siberian iris, *I. sibirica* (AGM) requires a good, moist soil; it will not grow in waterlogged conditions. It reaches around 36in (90cm) and has long, narrow leaves, with the flowers held well clear of the foliage on strong stems. There are a considerable number of named varieties, many with blue flowers, together with white and yellow. An ideal location is at the side of a pond or stream, although they will settle down happily in a border provided sufficient moisture is available.

One of the most impressive moisture lovers is the summer-flowering Japanese iris, *I. ensata* (AGM), formerly listed as *I. kaempferi*. This plant dislikes a limy or chalky soil. There are a whole host of named varieties with new additions being introduced, many from Japan where these plants are immensely popular. The flat flowers can be up to 8in (20cm) across, single or double, single coloured, or blended or netted with different coloured veining. One that has become very popular is 'Pink Frost'. Others to look out for are those with the 'Rowden' prefix. Many cultivars of *I. ensata* have retained the Japanese names, often considered by Westerners to be difficult to say or spell.

A real beauty that flowers in the depths of winter is the Algerian iris, *I. unguicularis* (AGM). Two of the best varieties to look out for are 'Mary Barnard' and 'Palette' – the latter, as its name indicates, comprises a mixture of several colours

Where to grow: All of the iris mentioned above require a sunny position. The tall

ABOVE *Iris* 'Dreaming Yellow': a variety of *Iris sibirica*

I. sibirica requires a plentiful supply of moisture, but should be grown at the side of a water feature, not in waterlogged conditions. It is most important that *I. ensata* has acid soil. As for *I. unguicularis*, this requires a sheltered position in full sun, ideally at the base of a sunny wall. The flowers require shelter during the winter while the rhizomes require baking in summer if they are to flower well

How to grow: Good, humus-rich, well-drained soil. The bearded iris prefers slightly alkaline conditions. Planting can be carried out in late summer or at other times in suitable weather and soil conditions, if plants are container-grown. The 'Algerian' iris should be planted in late winter or early spring

Flowering period: Early and mid-summer, with the exception of *I. unguicularis*, which flowers in early and mid-winter

Maintenance: Remove dead flower stems. Lift and divide every few years to maintain strong healthy growth and good flowering

bearded kinds can be grown in a bed of their own, or among other perennial plants. The dwarf bearded types, because of their stature, are ideal for a pocket on the rock garden. *I. pseudacorus* will grow in boggy conditions or shallow water.

ABOVE *Iris bucharica*: one of the easiest of the Juno group

ABOVE *Iris pseudacorus*: the well-known 'Yellow flag'

ABOVE *Iris sibirica* loves a moist spot

Propagation: Division after flowering
Pests and diseases: Slugs and snails can
be troublesome, especially on new growth

BULBOUS IRIS
Description: There are three main groups
of iris that fall within this section. First to
flower are those in the Reticulata group,
followed by the Xiphiums (better known to
many as the Dutch and Spanish irises), and
then the Juno irises.

Popular species and varieties: The first of
the Reticulata irises will bloom in late winter
and early spring, especially if the winter is
a mild one, and they are often to be seen in
flower at the same time as crocus. Among
the best is *Iris danfordiae*, with lovely deep
yellow flowers with green spots in the throat.
This is soon followed by *I. histrioides* 'Major'
(AGM), with its rich blue flowers just 6in
(15cm) high.

Late winter is a time when the dwarf irises
are at their best. Many gardeners will know
the old favourite *I. reticulata* (AGM) with its
deep mauve flowers highlighted by gold
markings on the falls. There are a number of
named varieties, including 'Cantab', a lovely

available in a range of colours, mainly shades of yellow, blue and white. Flowering takes place in early summer for the Dutch irises, with the Spanish irises following in mid-summer.

The Juno irises, of which there are some 50 or so species, are so distinct that some botanists have even classified them in their own Juno genus. The bulbs are usually small, and accompanied by thick, fleshy roots which help the bulbs to survive during the dormant season. Care is needed not to damage these roots during transplanting. One of the easiest is *I. bucharica*, an ideal subject for an alpine house or a very sheltered spot. The flowers comprise creamy white crests and bright yellow falls, and are carried several to an 18in (45cm) stem in mid-spring

pale blue; 'Harmony', a real gem with sky blue flowers; 'Joyce' is the same but with an orange-red ridge on its falls. 'J.S. Dijt' has distinctive reddish-purple blooms, and 'Pauline' is a dusky violet-pink highlighted by a large white spot on its falls. It would be all too easy to regard the creamy flowers overlaid with a blend of light yellow and curious greenish-blue of 'Katherine Hodgkin' (AGM) as being unsuitable for outside. It does, in fact, stand up well to outdoor conditions, if given a good, peaty soil.

The Xiphium irises are valuable garden plants with long-lasting qualities. They grow to 24–30in (60–75cm) in height and are

RIGHT *Iris* 'Pink Taffeta': a splendid tall bearded iris

ABOVE *Iris* 'Bright Eyes': an attractive dwarf iris

Where to grow: The Reticulata irises are ideal for planting in groups at the front of a border or in a pocket on the rock garden. They also make good subjects for pans in an alpine or cold greenhouse. The Dutch irises are excellent subjects for a border, again planted in groups
How to grow: Good, humus-rich soil in an open, sunny spot is preferred. Plant the bulbs in early autumn. The Reticulatas should be set 3in (7.5cm) deep and 4in (10cm) apart; the Xiphiums should be slightly deeper at 4–6in (10–15cm) and 6in (15cm) apart. The Junos should be handled with care so not to damage the brittle fleshy roots; plant 2in (5cm) deep
Flowering period: Recticulatas flower from mid- to late winter; the Juno and Xiphium groups bloom in early and mid-summer
Maintenance: Remove foliage after it has died back, otherwise leave the plants undisturbed
Propagation: Division in autumn
Pests and diseases: Ink disease can cause problems resulting in black spots on bulbs and foliage; when seen you should lift and destroy the bulbs. Blue mould can attack stored bulbs; again these should be destroyed when the condition is noticed. There are also other virus and fungal diseases that can attack bulbous iris

NAME: *LACHENALIA* (CAPE COWSLIP)
FAMILY: HYACINTHACEAE

Description: *Lachenalia* is another genus of bulbs originating from South Africa. These are splendid plants for the greenhouse or conservatory and are excellent for a bright windowsill as they will stand direct sun for part of the day. Lachenalias are noted for their neat, dense spikes of bell-shaped tubular flowers
Popular species and varieties: Although there are a number of species available, it is *L. aloides* that is the most frequently seen. The glaucous foliage is usually marked with blotches of green or purple. The flowers are yellow with red tips. There are several forms, including 'Aurea' (AGM), a plain golden yellow, 'Nelsonii' with blooms of soft yellow and green, and 'Quadricolor' (AGM) that has flowers of orange, yellow, green and purplish-red
Where to grow: These are not hardy, but are splendid subjects for the conservatory and greenhouse or in the home (however, they do not like centrally heated rooms)
How to grow: In late summer and early autumn plant six bulbs in a 5in (12.5cm) pot, using John Innes no. 2 compost with added coarse sand. The bulbs should be set

ABOVE *Lachenalia aloides*: widely known as Cape Cowslip

just below the surface. Take care not to over-water as this can lead to rotting

Flowering period: Early and mid-spring

Maintenance: Start to withhold water in early summer, and allow the pot to dry out until the autumn. This is the time to carefully remove the bulbs and repot them in fresh compost

Propagation: Detach offsets at repotting time. Pot these up using the same type of compost. Flowering size should be reached in two years

Pests and diseases: Lachenalias can fall victim to basal rot, resulting in the loss of the bulb

109

ABOVE *Leucojum vernum*: the spring snowflake

NAME: *LEUCOJUM* (SNOWFLAKE)
FAMILY: **AMARYLLIDACEAE**

Description: The spring snowflake, *Leucojum vernum* (AGM), flowers at the same time as snowdrops, which they resemble in some ways. Both belong to the same plant family. Look closely at leucojums and the difference is easily seen: the bell-shaped flowers have six petals of equal length, as opposed to those of the snowdrop which vary in length.

There are three types of snowflake, in the main referred to as the spring, summer and autumn snowflakes. The latter, *L. autumnale* (AGM), is best grown on the rock garden

Popular species and varieties: For many it is the spring snowflake with its pretty, pure white bell-shaped flowers, usually tipped with green, on 4–8in (10–20cm) high stems, that have the most appeal. The foliage is glossy,

mid-green and strap shaped, fairly compact when in flower but lengthening later.

Despite its name, the summer snowflake, *Leucojum aestivum*, normally flowers in late spring. This is a taller, more robust plant that can, in ideal conditions, reach 36in (90cm) in height; the stems carry umbels of white bell-shaped flowers tipped with green. In many ways the bulbs and foliage resemble that of daffodils. Look out for the form 'Gravetye Giant' (AGM), which has larger flowers and is a more robust plant generally.

Leucojum autumnale (AGM), the autumn snowflake, is a neat, delightful species reaching no more than 6in (15cm), with fine, narrow foliage. The thread-like stems carry up to four small white, pendent-bell shaped flowers

ABOVE *Leucojum nicaeense*: best grown on the rock garden

Where to grow: The spring and summer snowflakes enjoy cool moist soil.

Leucojum vernum (AGM) should be in a position where the soil does not dry out and become too hot in the summer. The summer snowflake is best in a lightly shaded spot; it looks particularly attractive in groups alongside a stream or pond. It can be naturalized in a wildlife garden. The autumn snowflake is best on the rock garden

How to grow: Planting should be carried out in late summer or early autumn with *L. vernum* and *L. autumnale*, setting the bulbs at a depth of 3in (7.5cm) and 4–8in (10–20cm) apart. *Leucojum aestivum* requires deeper planting, at 6in (15cm). Once in place they should be left

undisturbed for several years. All, with the exception of *L. autumnale*, do best in light, moist, humus-rich, well-drained soil

Flowering period: Early to late spring and autumn, depending on the species grown

Maintenance: Little is required. Remove dead foliage after it has died back. A top-dressing of well-rotted compost at this time is beneficial

Propagation: Lift and divide clumps while in growth, during spring or early summer; replant immediately. Leucojums can also be grown from seed. This is a lengthy process, taking several years before the young bulbs are large enough to produce flowers

Pests and diseases: Generally no problems

111

ABOVE *Lilium* 'Grand Cru': dynamic appearance – Asiatic hybrid

NAME: *LILIUM (LILY)*
FAMILY: LILIACEAE

Description: The lily family consists of several groups and sub-divisions covering the enormous range of types available. Lilies include some of the most beautiful and stately bulbous plants, with flowers in numerous different forms from outward-facing blooms, to trumpet-shaped, flattish, and some referred to as Turk's cap lilies, with pendent blooms.

Lilies are perfect in groups in a border, among shrubs, or in patio containers. An ideal situation is a sunny position protected from strong wind, and where they can receive light shading for part of the day – especially to the roots. Many lilies are fragrant, so these should be positioned where they can be enjoyed to the full

Popular species and varieties: One lily species that has a very long history of cultivation is the Madonna lily, *Lilium candidum* (AGM). It produces 4ft (1.2m) high, strong stems in early summer and carries fragrant, pure white funnel-shaped flowers that can be up to 6in (15cm) wide. This lily requires a warm, sheltered position. It is basal rooting, and can sometimes be difficult to establish. Once planted, leave it undisturbed.

Another well-known lily is the regal lily, *L. regale* (AGM). This is certainly one of the best white funnel-shaped lilies. Its fragrant blooms in mid-summer can be 6in (15cm) long, with several on a stout stem. This is a sun lover, happy in moist soils and noted for its ability to increase quickly.

Lilium lancifolium (which until recently was known universally as *L. tigrinum*) is commonly known as the tiger lily. It has dark orange blooms with black spots, carried on stems 2–5ft (60–150cm) high.

Lilium martagon, widely known as the Turk's cap or Martagon lily, also has a long history in cultivation. It grows to 5ft (1.5m), and its leaves are arranged in whorls at regular intervals along its stem. The flowers are rose-purple with dark spots; the petals are reflexed, giving them a Turk's cap shape. It is a very hardy species, and is good for naturalizing among shrubs or in grassy areas. *L. martagon* is basal rooting, and over the years has been a parent to numerous hybrids, including a lovely white form, 'Album' (AGM).

One that should not be overlooked is the golden-rayed lily, *L. auratum*. A native of Japan, it has white, fragrant, saucer-shaped flowers, each petal of which has a distinct yellow band running along its length. This is a lime-hating species, and is perhaps best grown in a container.

Look out also for *L. auratum* var. *platyphyllum* (AGM), with large, waxy, white flowers.

ABOVE *Lilium regale*: one of the best white trumpet lilies

BELOW *Lilium* 'Arena': strong-growing oriental hybrid

ABOVE *Lilium* 'Stargazer': great favourite among the Oriental hybrids

Look out also for the pollen-free semi-double buttercup yellow 'Fata Morgana'; the centre of each bloom has maroon dots.

The Oriental hybrid lilies boast some excellent varieties among their number, many of which are fragrant. They flower from mid-summer onwards. They are lime haters, so if your soil is alkaline grow them in containers. Among the best are 'Arena', large white flowers with a yellow star in the centre, and 'Casa Blanco' (AGM), white with blooms 8in (20cm) or more across. Two others, both well known, are 'Stargazer', a rich crimson edged with white and liberally spotted with maroon, and 'Bergamo', rich pink with yellow midribs.

Then there are the Trumpet lilies. These majestic bulbs are an asset to any garden, with their stout stems and large trumpet-shaped flowers. Most bloom in mid-summer. One that comes highly recommended is the deep yellow 'Golden Splendour', its huge flowers being held on 5ft (1.5m) stems. 'African Queen' is another to look out for, its rich pink-orange buds open to glossy, glowing orange trumpets.

There are also lilies of dwarf stature, splendid subjects for patio containers, growing to just 12–15in (30–40cm). Among them are 'Crimson Pixie', a glowing crimson, 'Lemon Pixie' with soft yellow flowers, and 'Buff Pixie', a golden peach colour

Where to grow: Lilies are good border plants. Interplant them among perennials or shrubs. The Orientals are lime haters, although they can be grown perfectly well in containers using ericaceous compost. The same applies to some of the species

How to grow: Choose a sunny or lightly shaded position sheltered from the wind and with good humus-rich soil. Plant in groups, between 4–9in (10–23cm) deep, depending on size of the bulb, and 9–15in (23–38cm) apart. This can be done in autumn or early spring. Take care not to bruise or damage the bulbs when handling, and plant as soon as possible

Many more splendid species lilies are available, and it is best to contact a specialist before making your choice.

There are hundreds of hybrid lilies, and some of the most dramatic are in the group known as the Asiatics. These are arguably the easiest to grow, and they produce sturdy growth with stems some 36–48in (90–120cm) high, and upward-facing blooms. Flowering is from early to mid-summer. These are splendid subjects for beds and borders and are also excellent in pots and patio containers. The best varieties include 'Grand Cru', an eye-catching deep yellow with each petal distinctly marked with deep red, 'Fire King' with brilliant orange-red flowers and purple dots, and 'Montreux', a lovely deep pink with light spots towards the centre. One that stands out is 'Lollipop', a cream-white with petal tips of raspberry pink.

Flowering period: Summer, the precise timing depends on type grown

Maintenance: There is no need to lift lilies for the winter. If after several years they show sign of decline, lift and divide them. You should plant in a fresh place, or replace some of the soil.

Mulching in spring, with well-rotted manure or compost is beneficial, as is feeding with a high-potash liquid fertilizer during the growing season. Lilies in containers should be moved under cover in severe weather. In exposed or cold areas it is a good idea to give winter protection to garden lilies, by covering the soil with dry bracken or conifer branches

Propagation: Lilies can be increased by division, bulbils, scales or offsets

Pests and diseases: Mice, rabbits and squirrels can attack new growth in the spring. Aphids can become a nuisance; they should be dealt with as soon as seen as they can transmit virus diseases. Fungus diseases and viruses can also attack lilies, causing mottling, spotting, stunted growth and other symptoms. Lift and destroy any infected plants

ABOVE *Lilium* 'Montreux': a pale Asiatic hybrid

ABOVE *Lilium* 'Royal Gold': a variety of *L. regale*

115

NAME: *MUSCARI* (GRAPE HYACINTH)
FAMILY: **HYACINTHACEAE**

Description: These are among the best known of all the spring-flowering bulbs. Anyone who has visited the famous Keukenhof Gardens at Lisse in Holland will surely remember the spectacular muscari plantings among the trees. The bulbs, with their flower heads of tiny bell-shaped blooms, include several species ideal for naturalizing under deciduous trees. Others are not so vigorous but are still most effective when planted in groups

Popular species and varieties: The most widely grown grape hyacinth is *Muscari armeniacum* (AGM), a native of southeast Europe and western Asia. The foliage spreads and separates as the flower spike develops; this reaches a height of 8in (20cm), with mid-blue bell-shaped, tightly packed flowers.

Another good species, this time from the mountains of Turkey, is *M. azureum* (AGM), which grows to 4–6in (10–15cm), with dense spikes of bright blue flowers. There is also a white form, 'Album'.

Also from Turkey comes *M. latifolium*, which produces one leaf from each bulb.

ABOVE *Muscari armeniacum*: the very popular grape hyacinth

ABOVE *Muscari latifolium*: this unusual species produces just one leaf per bulb

In early spring the unusual flowers appear on stems 8in (20cm) or more high. These are easily recognizable: the lower blooms are of a deep blackish-violet, and those towards the top are mid-blue and smaller.

Entirely different in appearance is the feather hyacinth, *M. comosum* 'Plumosum'. It is sterile; the heads consist entirely of minute branched blue filaments.

M. botryoides 'Album' is very neat and attractive; the compact, pure white, fragrant flowers are held on 6in (15cm) long stems. It is a good choice for a sunny pocket on the rock garden

Where to grow: Muscari can be planted in numerous parts of the garden, in groups, beds, borders, pockets on the rock garden and in patio containers. Many forms are ideal for naturalizing

How to grow: Plant in groups in late summer or early autumn, in good humus-rich conditions. Set the bulbs 3in (7.5cm) deep and 4in (10cm) apart

Flowering period: Early to mid-spring

Maintenance: A light dressing of a good general fertilizer after flowering helps to build up the bulbs. Additional feeding is not generally necessary. Lift and divide bulbs every three to four years

Propagation: Lift the bulb after flowering; replant immediately

Pests and diseases: No problems are usually experienced with these bulbs

NAME: *NARCISSUS* (DAFFODIL)
FAMILY: AMARYLLIDACEAE

Description: If any plant indicates the arrival of spring it is the daffodil, one of the most popular of all spring bulbs. Forms of *Narcissus* have been grouped into 13 divisions, due to the wide variety of types available. Unless you are naturalizing, it is best to avoid mixtures due to the differing flowering times. Far better results are obtained by grouping the same variety. Even if you have a small garden there are the miniature trumpet daffodils that can be grown in a small bed or in patio containers

Popular species and varieties: The best-known daffodils are unquestionably the Trumpet types, which include the deep yellow 'Golden Harvest', 'Dutch Master' (AGM) and 'Rembrandt'. There is also the very popular, nicely formed, white-flowered 'Mount Hood' (AGM), and the lovely white and yellow 'Bravoure' (AGM).

Another popular group is the large cup *Narcissus*, including the clear yellow 'Carlton' (AGM) and old favourite 'Spellbinder' (AGM) with yellow petals and sulphur-lemon cup. One that always stands out is 'Carbineer', a flower of great substance with its broad golden-yellow perianth and bright orange cup. One of my favourites in this group is 'Saint Keverne'

ABOVE *Narcissus* 'Jack Snipe': free-flowering member of the Cyclamineus group

(AGM) with a clear yellow perianth and cup that stands up well to wind and rain. There are many more excellent varieties in this group.

Many beauties exist among the small cupped narcissus. Try 'Barrett Browning', with a pure white perianth highlighted by a short, deep orange-red cup. Equally dramatic is 'Sabine Hay', with neat, light orange perianth and small orange cup.

The double daffodils may not be to everyone's taste, but this group does include some splendid varieties. Among them are 'Tahiti' (AGM) with neat overlapping golden-yellow petals interspersed with smaller petals of bright orange in the centre of the flower. Look out for 'Unique' (AGM), its neat blooms of pure white made even more attractive by interspersed smaller petals of chrome yellow.

Group five comprises the *Triandrus narcissi*. These are not as tall, ranging from 8–15in (20–38cm). 'Hawera' (AGM) produces two or three small, drooping flowers on an 8in (20cm) stem; each bloom comprises a bell-shaped crown and reflexing petals of soft cream-yellow. Also with several flowers on a stem is 'Rippling Waters', which has a cup and perianth of pure white.

Group six is the Cyclamineus group, noted for flowers with reflexed petals, in many ways resembling those of *Cyclamen*. One of the best known is 'February Gold', highly regarded for its early flowering. It grows to just 12in (30cm) and produces a yellow perianth and golden-yellow trumpet. One of my favourites is 'Jetfire' (AGM), the golden reflexed petals a perfect foil for the long, orange trumpets held on 10in (25cm) tall stems.

ABOVE *Narcissus* 'Spellbinder': an excellent all round trumpet daffodil

One of the first daffodils to flower is 'Peeping Tom' (AGM); an intense golden yellow, it brightens up any garden. The trumpets are long and have an attractive rolled edge making this a variety easy to identify.

In recent years the dwarf daffodils have become very popular due mainly to their resistance to strong winds. 'Baby Moon', a member of the Jonquilla narcissus group, produces deep yellow flowers on 6in (15cm) stems, in clusters of up to three on a stem. It is noted for its late season and free-flowering habits.

The 'Tazetta' group usually produces several stems on each bulb. Most are fragrant with well-formed blooms. One to look out for is 'Scarlet Gem', with its golden-yellow perianth and brilliant orange-scarlet cup. It has a neat habit and grows to 15in (38cm) in height.

Group ten comprises the species and wild forms of narcissus. Among these are the yellow hoop petticoat narcissus, *N. bulbocodium* (AGM), and the Lent lily, *N. pseudonarcissus*. A fine subject for naturalizing, this latter form does take a few seasons to become established. Late spring is when *N. poeticus* comes into bloom. Many will know this as the pheasant's eye narcissus; the flowers are white with a small yellow cup and a bright orange or red rim. This is a good subject for planting in grass.

The remaining divisions include the split coronas types, and also those that do not fit into any of the other groups. Here you will find 'Tete a Tete' (AGM), a splendid, very popular variety that produces two or three of its golden-yellow blooms on 6in (15cm) high stems

Where to grow: Beds or borders, with the dwarf varieties ideal for tubs and containers or on the

rock garden. Daffodils grow and flower well in grassland or under deciduous trees, where they may be left undisturbed for years. When growing in beds or borders, planting baskets can be used. After flowering has finished, lift and replant elsewhere and your bed or border is ready for the summer-flowering subjects

How to grow: Daffodils fare best growing in well-drained heavier loams, but they will also grow in many other types of soil, provided they are not waterlogged. Avoid any freshly manured positions.

Plant in mid-summer, or as soon as possible after this: narcissus produce roots early. Set them in irregular groups of the same variety rather than in regimented lines. When naturalizing, scatter bulbs at random and plant where they fall, using a hand trowel or special bulb planter. The larger bulbs should have about 4in (10cm) of soil on top. In spots where they will remain throughout the year and are likely to be forked over, plant an inch or more deeper

Flowering period: Depending on variety, late winter to early spring

Maintenance: The bulbs must be left to die down naturally, with the foliage at least yellow before lifting. Under no circumstances should you knot the foliage – as has often been recommended in older gardening books – as this weakens the bulb by reducing the amount of leaf area exposed to the sun and in turn formation of food reserves in the bulb and production of flowers the following year.

After around three to four years lift, divide and replant the bulbs, this will avoid congestion and poor flowering. Where bulbs are planted in grass do not mow until at least six or seven weeks have passed since the flowers faded.

An application of a balanced general fertilizer applied in the spring, and lightly

LEFT *Narcissus* 'Tahiti': a double variety, overlapping golden petals, others smaller of orange-red

RIGHT *Nerine bowdenii:* flowers in the autumn

worked into the soil, is beneficial. Take care not to damage new growth. Water plants well in hot, dry spells

Propagation: Divide after flowering

Pests and diseases: Basal rot can cause bulbs to become soft. Destroy any in this condition. Stem and bulb eelworm causes distortion and twisting of the foliage; lift and destroy the bulbs. Grubs of the narcissus fly tunnel into the bulbs causing them to produce numerous thin leaves and no flowers. Again you should lift and destroy the bulbs.

There are several viral diseases that can attack narcissus; those affected may show signs of mottling or discoloration of the foliage, together with a general decline in flowering. There is no cure, so again you should lift and destroy

NAME: *NERINE* (GUERNSEY LILY)
FAMILY: **AMARYLLIDACEAE**

Description: Several species of *Nerine* are half hardy, which means that they will need protection from cold in winter, but one exception is *Nerine bowdenii* (AGM). This can be grown in a sheltered spot, ideally at the foot of a sunny wall, and adds colour to the autumn garden. Nerines are native to South Africa.

One species, *N. sarniensis*, is surrounded with mystery. It would seem that its connection with the UK Channel Island of Guernsey goes back to the mid-1600s when it was thought that members of a ship's crew gave bulbs to a local landowner. Since then the plants have become naturalized on the island. Nerines flower best when well established. A hot, dry summer will also improve their display

Popular species and varieties: The long-lasting, bright pink flower heads of *N. bowdenii* (AGM) appear before the foliage. Each 18–24in (45–60cm) long stem carries up to 12 blooms with undulating petals. They can be left undisturbed for several years.

Nerine flexuosa is not as tall, growing to 12in (30cm), but produces lovely pink umbels. Each bloom has narrow reflexed and crinkled petals. There is also a white form available listed as 'Alba'.

The Guernsey lily, *N. sarniensis*, produces bright scarlet flowers on 18in (45cm) stems. Due to its vibrant colouring it has been used to produce some of the excellent hybrids available. Neither *N. flexuosa* nor *N. sarniensis* are hardy

Where to grow: Only one, *N. bowdenii* (AGM) can be relied upon to grow outside, and even then it can be damaged in very severe winters. The others are best grown as pot plants, and brought under cover for winter

How to grow: Plant the bulbs of *N. bowdenii* in mid-summer or late spring in good humus-rich, well-drained soil, in a sheltered spot. Plant them 4in (10cm) deep and allow 6in (15cm) between them. The neck of the bulb should be at, or just below, soil level.

When grown in pots, place three bulbs in a 6in (15cm) pot containing John Innes no. 2 compost. Again, the neck of the bulb should be just visible. Water the bulbs but do not apply more water until the buds appear. Keep the compost just moist throughout the winter. Place the container in a heated greenhouse or conservatory, with a minimum temperature of 50°F (10°C). Feed every two weeks with a weak liquid fertilizer when the buds first appear, and continue with this until the flowers have finished and the foliage starts to die down. Withhold water from this time until growth starts again

Flowering period: Late summer to early autumn

Maintenance: *Nerine bowdenii* does not require a rich soil, as this encourages foliage rather than flowers. Remove dead stems. Apply a mulch of peat in late autumn to help protect the bulbs over winter

Propagation: Remove offsets and grow on. Alternatively, grow from seed – this will take at least three years before the resulting bulbs reach flowering size

Pests and diseases: Mealy bug can become troublesome under glass; treat it immediately with a suitable systemic insecticide. A virus disease causing yellow and mottled foliage can attack nerines; destroy any plants affected

ABOVE *Ornithogalum umbellatum*: known by the common name Star of Bethlehem

NAME: *ORNITHOGALUM* (STAR OF BETHLEHEM)
FAMILY: HYACINTHACEAE

Description: The best-known member of this family is unquestionably the Star of Bethlehem, *Ornithogalum umbellatum*. It has been grown in our gardens for a great many years and has become a firm favourite of cottage gardens, where it can often be seen lining the edge of a border or path. For most of the year it lies forgotten, until its heads of numerous flowers appear in mid-spring

Popular species and varieties: In nature, *O. umbellatum* has a very wide distribution; it is found in Europe, Asia and North Africa. A very hardy and free-flowering plant, with glistening white flowers held over grassy foliage.

The blooms of *O. nutans* (AGM) are white and green and are larger, pendent and bell shaped; they are held on 6–10in (15–25cm) high stems. This is a good plant for naturalizing under trees.

The Chincherinchee, *O. thyrsoides*, which is widely known as a flower for florists, is not hardy and must be grown in pots

Where to grow: The hardy members of the family are happy in ordinary, well-drained soil in beds or borders, on the rock garden or in short grass. Most are sun lovers, but *O. nutans* will grow in light shade

How to grow: The bulbs can be planted in spring or autumn, and should be set at a depth of 2in (5cm), and about 10–12in (20–30cm) apart. Feeding is not required unless the bulbs are being grown in very poor soil. Plant in groups for best effect

Flowering period: Mid-spring to early summer

Maintenance: Little is required except to remove dead flower stems and foliage after it has died back

Propagation: Lift and divide bulbs after flowering; replant immediately

Pests and diseases: No problems are usually encountered with these bulbs

NAME: *OXALIS* (WOOD SORREL)
FAMILY: **OXALIDACEAE**

Description: This is a huge family with over 800 species, some of which are very invasive. There are a number that are excellent garden plants, however. These are generally sun lovers, and most have clover-like foliage

Popular species and varieties: One of the easiest of this family is *Oxalis adenophylla* (AGM), a native of Chile. It produces a rather unusual bulb-like rhizome that has a fibre coating. Its dwarf habit, growing to just 4in (10cm), makes it a good subject for the rock garden. In spring it produces a neat rosette of crinkled grey-green leaves, which are soon followed by the satin-pink flowers some 1in (2.5cm) across and held on long stems.

Also from Chile is *O. lobata*, with a curious growth habit. In spring, tufts of bright green foliage first appear, and then disappear, which can easily lead to one thinking that the plant has died. In the autumn it returns, this time short-stemmed flowers of pure golden yellow accompany the leaves. It is a good plant for the alpine house, as is *O. obtusa*, which produces tufts of trifoliate leaves and wide funnel-shaped blooms of a rich rose-pink.

One very colourful oxalis that is happy in a sunny spot where it receives some shelter from a wall is *O. depressa*, a free-flowering plant with masses of bright rose-pink flowers over grey-green foliage

Where to grow: Oxalis grown on a rock garden require a sunny spot in well-drained, humus-rich soil. *Oxalis lobata* and *O. obtusa* are alpine house subjects that, when not in flower, can spend the summer in a frame. *Oxalis depressa* can be slightly invasive, ideal for around steps and as an edging to borders.

ABOVE *Oxalis depressa*: masses of flowers in early summer

It can be checked in severe winters, but usually recovers satisfactorily

How to grow: *Oxalis adenophylla* and *O. depressa* should be planted in groups in gritty, well-drained, humus-rich soil, with the bulb set just below the surface. Oxalis growing under glass also require a good draining, gritty, loam-based compost. Top-dress the pots with coarse grit to prevent the loamy soil from forming a 'pan' over the bulbs

Flowering period: It depends on the species – early summer for *O. adenophylla*, mid-summer for *O. depressa*, and late summer to early autumn for *O. lobata*

Maintenance: There is little required, except for the removal of dead foliage

Propagation: Divide the bulb-like rhizomes after flowering; replant immediately

Pests and diseases: Generally trouble-free

ABOVE *Oxalis adenophylla*: flowers in early summer, ideal for the rock garden

BELOW *Oxalis lobata*: a plant with curious habits

NAME: *RANUNCULUS* (PERSIAN BUTTERCUP)
FAMILY: **RANUNCULACEAE**

Description: One of the characteristics of *Ranunculus asiaticus*, and the various hybrids derived from it, is the brightness of their colours. The species originates from the eastern Mediterranean regions, and produces unusual-shaped tubers. In addition to the single-flowered wild species are the cultivated semi-double and double forms

Popular species and varieties: *Ranunculus asiaticus* produces saucer-shaped blooms with a central mass of stamens. Colours range from a dazzling red to bright yellow with pink, orange and white. The semi- and fully double types are the most popular and are normally sold as mixtures. The singles are often to be found listed in catalogues of nurserymen specializing in alpine plants

Where to grow: Ranunculus are sun lovers requiring a sheltered position at the foot of a wall, in groups among shrubs, or in a border

How to grow: Plant the claw-like tubers 1–2in (2.5–5cm) deep, and 6in (15cm) apart, in the

RIGHT *Ranunculus* 'Acolade': a popular double-flowered variety

BELOW *Ranunculus asiaticus*: requires a sunny well-drained spot

spring. The bulbs can become dry and, if this is the case, it is a good idea to soak them in tepid water for a few hours before planting. The soil should be well drained; incorporate well-rotted compost a few weeks before planting. In ideal conditions they will survive for several seasons

Flowering period: Late spring to early summer
Maintenance: In many areas it is best to lift the tubers after they have died back. Clean them and store for the winter in dry peat in a frost-free place; replant in the spring. After three or four seasons they should be replaced with new stock

Propagation: In the spring, carefully divide the tubers before replanting
Pests and diseases: Normally, no problems are experienced with these tuberous plants

ABOVE *Rhodohypoxis 'Tetra'*: best grown in an alpine house or a very sheltered, sunny, well-drained pocket on the rock garden

NAME: *RHODOHYPOXIS* (ROSE GRASS)
FAMILY: HYPOXIDACEAE

Description: The low-growing free-flowering *Rhodohypoxis* is native to the Cape region of South Africa. These are excellent subjects for the alpine house and can be grown outside in sheltered, lime-free, well-drained conditions. Colours range from a rich rose-red through shades of pink, together with white-flowered varieties. All have six petals in two sets of three, one on top of the other, meeting at the centre, resulting in no visible 'eye' to the flower

Popular species and varieties: *Rhodohypoxis baurii* (AGM) grows to 4in (10cm) in height, with narrow, hairy grass-like leaves. There are many named forms, among them the rich pink 'Fred Broome', with 'Albrighton' a deeper pink, and 'Appleblossom' a blush pink. The reds include 'Douglas' and 'Monty'. Among the whites are 'Picta', the petals of which have pink tips, and 'Ruth'

Where to grow: When grown outside, choose a sheltered, sunny spot, ideally a pocket on the rock garden or at the edge of a border. In cold districts lift them for the winter, or grow them in pots in an alpine house or cold greenhouse

How to grow: These colourful plants require lime-free conditions, moisture-retentive but well-drained soil. They will not tolerate cold, wet soils and are excellent subjects for pots if grown in a gritty mixture top-dressed with chippings. Plant the tubers 2in (5cm) deep and 4in (10cm) apart

Flowering period: Late spring, and throughout the summer months

Maintenance: Rhodohypoxis are dormant during the winter, so when grown outside their position should be marked to avoid accidental damage. In the winter try to shelter them from excessive wet by placing a well-supported pane of glass or a cloche over them. Those grown in pots should be repotted in early spring. Water the plants well during the growing period. In cold areas, lift and store the tubers in dry peat in a frost-free place

Propagation: Lift and divide offsets in the autumn; replant immediately

Pests and diseases: Generally no problems

NAME: *ROMULEA*
FAMILY: **IRIDACEAE**

Description: These small plants, with their grassy foliage, in many ways resemble crocus. They are not difficult to grow, provided a few simple requirements are met. They are not often seen in our gardens

Popular species and varieties: *Romulea bulbocodium* is the most reliable species, growing to 2–4in (5–10cm) in height. It is a variable plant with funnel-shaped lilac-blue flowers in early spring. These open wide in full sun, but remain closed in dull conditions

Where to grow: Choose an open, warm spot where Romulea can enjoy sun throughout the day. A pocket on the rock garden is ideal; alternatively, grow them in an alpine house

How to grow: The soil should be good, and well drained. Plant in the autumn, about 2in (5cm) deep, and leave them undisturbed, to build them up into a clump. Flowering improves considerably during this time

Flowering period: Early spring

ABOVE *Romulea bulbocodium*: needs a warm sunny, well-drained spot

131

Maintenance: It is not usually necessary to feed them, unless they are growing in a poor soil. Water the plants freely in hot weather during the growing season. Remove any dead foliage after the plants have died back. It is a good idea to mark the spot to avoid any accidental damage

Propagation: Carefully lift and divide the plants after flowering; replant immediately. Romulea can also be grown from seed but, like many bulbous plants, take some time to reach flowering size

Pests and diseases: Generally trouble-free. Birds can damage the flowers; protect if necessary

NAME: *SCADOXUS* (BLOOD LILY)
FAMILY: **AMARYLLIDACEAE**

Description: The *Scadoxus* is a bulbous plant that is often still found listed in catalogues and garden centres under its old name of *Haemanthus*. It is a very showy plant for the greenhouse or conservatory

Popular species and varieties: *Scadoxus multiflorus* is a native of South Africa. As its name implies, it produces a rounded head comprised of 200 or more small red flowers, each with long protruding stamens. The head is carried on a stout 12in (30cm) tall stem, accompanied by bright green foliage

Where to grow: As a pot plant in the home, greenhouse or conservatory

How to grow: Plant in the early spring, in a 6in (15cm) pot, using John Innes no. 2 compost. Set the bulb so that its tip is just level with the surface. Keep it in a warm place at around 55–61°F (13–16°C). When in active growth, keep it well watered and feed it every two weeks with a high-potash liquid fertilizer. These bulbs should be left undisturbed for as long as possible. They flower best when slightly pot-bound

Flowering period: Late spring and the early summer period

Maintenance: When the foliage starts to turn yellow, withhold water, dry off the bulb in its pot. In mid-winter remove some of the top compost, taking care not to disturb the bulb, and then replace it with fresh

Propagation: Carefully remove offsets in the spring and grow these on. Take care not to disturb the 'mother' bulb too much. It will be some time before the offsets reach flowering size

Pests and diseases: Usually no problems are experienced with these bulbs

LEFT *Scadoxus multiflorus*: the impressive blood lily is native to South Africa

NAME: *SCHIZOSTYLIS* (KAFFIR LILY)
FAMILY: **IRIDACEAE**

Description: Mid-autumn is a time when colour is particularly welcome in the border as most of the summer-flowering perennials are well past their best. This is when the colourful *Schizostylis* grows from fleshy rhizomes to produce its gladiolus-like flowers, over tall, grassy foliage.

Native to South Africa, this plant requires a sunny, sheltered position but also moist soil during the summer. It is also good for cutting and bringing indoors

Popular species and varieties: *Schizostylis coccinea* is widely available; it produces up to ten bright scarlet star-shaped blooms on wiry 30in (75cm) long stems. There are a whole host of named varieties; among the best known is 'Major' (AGM) having larger deep red flowers on stronger stems. Also noted for its vigorous habit is 'Vicountess Byng', an attractive pale pink. With flowers of salmon pink, 'Sunrise' (AGM) is one not to overlook, as is the deep salmon 'Zeal Salmon', the flowers of which stand up well to any inclement weather. To add contrast, the lovely *Schizostylis coccinea alba* is another good selection. New varieties are still making their debut, one of the latest being 'Pink Princess' (AGM) with large, very pale pink flowers

Where to grow: These plants are suitable for mixed borders or a place in the garden where their late flowers can be seen to full advantage. Choose gritty, humus-rich soil in a sheltered, sunny or lightly shaded position, where they will not dry out during the summer. They are not suitable for cold, exposed gardens, but can be grown under glass

How to grow: Plant the rhizomes in late winter, 2in (5cm) deep and 12in (30cm) apart. They are vigorous subjects and require division every two or three years otherwise they will not flower as freely

ABOVE *Schizostylis* 'Major': useful for their late flowers

Flowering period: Late summer to mid-autumn, depending on the variety

Maintenance: In early winter, cut down dead growth and protect the bulbs with a layer of straw or bracken. In late winter or early spring, a mulch of peat or well-rotted compost will help to retain moisture

Propagation: Lift and carefully divide the clumps in early spring. Ensure each piece has five or six shoots; replant immediately

Pests and diseases: A fungal disease causing red-brown rust-like marks can attack the foliage, and in some cases flower buds. Caterpillars of the swift moth, and millipedes, can attack the roots

NAME: *SCILLA* (SQUILL)
FAMILY: **HYACINTHACEAE**

Description: In mid-winter the buds of *Scilla mischtschenkoana* appear and, depending on the season, can be in flower at the same time as aconites and snowdrops. In due course this plant is followed by other members of its family, including the best known of all, *Scilla siberica* (AGM) – see below

Popular species and varieties: The ideal starting point is the first to flower, albeit with an almost unpronounceable name. *Scilla mischtschenkoana* has pale blue flowers with a deeper blue stripe on each petal. It grows to 6in (15cm) in height and, like so many bulbs, is best planted in groups.

Just as this is going over, the dainty *S. bifolia* (AGM) comes into flower. As its name indicates it produces two leaves; they are strap shaped, and open out to allow the 4in (10cm) stem, usually carrying up to ten blue star-shaped flowers, to appear in late winter. The leaves remain short until flowering finishes then, as with *S. mischtschenkoana*, they lengthen. There is also a white form, *S. bifolia* 'Alba' and a purplish-pink *S. bifolia* 'Rosea'. This *Scilla* will often naturalize itself when growing in ideal conditions.

S. siberica (AGM) is a dwarf bulb from central and southern Russia, and is indispensable in the spring garden. Its leaves make their appearance in early spring and are soon followed by the 4in (10cm) stems carrying

RIGHT *Scilla mischtschenkoana*: an almost unpronounceable name, the first to flower

RIGHT *Sternbergia lutea*: autumn flowering

three or four blue, bell-shaped flowers. Look out for *S. siberica* 'Spring Beauty', a robust form with larger bright blue flowers. There is also a white form, 'Alba'.

Mid-spring is when the very attractive *Scilla peruviana* produces its strong 9–12in (22–30cm) tall stem carrying a head of numerous violet-blue star-shaped flowers

Where to grow: Scillas can be grown in a sunny place in the garden, but are best in a lightly shaded position at the edge of a border, or on the rock garden. They make excellent plants for pots in an alpine house

How to grow: Moist but well-drained, humus-rich soil. Plant the bulbs in early autumn, about 2in (5cm) deep, spacing them 4–6in (10–15cm) apart. They can be left undisturbed for three or four years. Sprinkling the area with a light dressing of a well-balanced fertilizer, or bone meal, carefully work into the soil after flowering, is beneficial

Flowering period: Early to mid-spring

Maintenance: Little is required except to remove any dead foliage after it has died back

Propagation: Offsets can be removed and the best time to do this is as the leaves die down. Clean, divide and replant the mature bulbs. The offsets can be planted in a nursery bed to grow on, usually taking three or so years to reach flowering size. Scillas can also be grown from seed; here again taking some time to reach flowering size

Pests and diseases: Bulb and stem eelworms can attack the bulbs, causing internal rotting

NAME: *STERNBERGIA* (AUTUMN DAFFODIL, LILY OF THE FIELD)
FAMILY: AMARYLLIDACEAE

Description: These are Mediterranean plants requiring hot, dry, sunny conditions; they thrive in light, sandy soils in a suitable pocket on the rock garden or in a bulb frame. Flowering in the autumn, they produce large bright yellow blooms, not unlike the *Crocus*

Popular species and varieties: The best-known species is *Sternbergia lutea*, which produces its strap-like glossy leaves and bright yellow funnel-shaped flowers in early autumn. It reaches 6–8in (15–20cm) in height. The slightly larger *S. clusiana* requires extra warmth in the summer, and winter protection,

and should be grown in a bulb frame
Where to grow: Ideally in a sunny, very
well-drained position on the rock garden,
or in a sheltered spot at the front of a border
How to grow: Plant the bulbs in the spring,
5in (12.5cm) deep and spaced at the same
distance. Incorporating coarse sand or grit is
beneficial, as is the addition of well-rotted
compost prior to planting; bulbs can rot

away in heavy or other unsuitable places.
Leave the bulbs undisturbed, so that they
may grow into sizeable clumps
Flowering period: Late summer and the early
autumn period
Maintenance: The foliage remains until the
spring, by which time it will have died back;
this is the time to remove the dead leaves.
Where possible, do not allow heavy summer

rain to ruin the flowers; protecting the plants with a cloche is one way to stop this
Propagation: Carefully divide the clumps in early autumn; replant immediately
Pests and diseases: Generally trouble-free

NAME: *TECOPHILAEA*
FAMILY: **TECOPHILIACEAE**

Description: Over the years much has been written about the intense, unrivalled blue of the spring gentian. One bulbous plant certainly has an equal claim, *Tecophilaea cyanocrocus* (AGM). It originates from the high alpine meadows of the Chilean Andes where sadly it is now thought to be extinct.

These are plants that require the winter protection of a cold greenhouse or an alpine house. Only a few years ago they were very difficult to obtain commercially but, thankfully, this has changed. They are, however, still rather expensive, due to their slow speed of increase. The Tecophilaea produces an almost flat corm, with a fine matted tunic.

They are not difficult to grow successfully, provided a few simple requirements are met
Popular species and varieties: *Tecophilaea cyanocrocus* has funnel-shaped, intense deep blue flowers with a whitish eye. There are two varieties – 'Leichtlini' (AGM) has flowers of a lighter blue, with prominent white centres, and 'Violacea' (occasionally found listed as 'Purpurea'), a deep violet-blue, very attractive but lacking the appeal of the previous two
Where to grow: These plants must be grown under glass, so that they are protected against severe weather
How to grow: Ideally grow them in clay pots, using a gritty, rich, loam-based compost, and top-dress this with coarse grit. Plant the bulbs in autumn, and plunge the pots to the rim in

ABOVE *Tecophilaea cyanocrocus*: the impressive Chilean crocus, a native of the Andes

138

ABOVE *Tigridia pavonia:* 'Tiger Flower', individual blooms are short-lived

coarse sand. Keep the compost moist through to early summer when the plants will start to die back; take care not to over-water. When the corms are dormant, water very sparingly, providing only enough to prevent the compost drying out completely

Flowering period: Late winter to early spring. If possible, purchase several mature corms together; when in flower, five or more produce a gorgeous display

Maintenance: Repot annually in early autumn

Propagation: After approximately five years, the corms will produce one offset annually. Carefully remove this offset, repot it and grow

it on. Even then it can take up to four years for the offsets to reach flowering size

Pests and diseases: Normally no problems are experienced with these plants

NAME: *TIGRIDIA* ('TIGER FLOWER')
FAMILY: **IRIDACEAE**

Description: The exotic blooms of this native South African plant last for just one day, but a succession of flowers quickly follow them, over a long period. The flowers have six petals, the three outer ones are large, with those on the inside carrying spots of a contrasting colour, making the flowers quite spectacular

139

Popular species and varieties: *Tigridia pavonia* is available in a range of brilliant colours and, as a result, is usually sold as a mixture. Some bulb suppliers do, however, list individual colours. Very few flowers are more picturesque, ranging from bright red, yellow, orange, lilac and pink through to white; all have the very distinctive heavily spotted centre

Where to grow: Choose a warm, sunny spot, sheltered from the wind. Tigridias grow to 18in (45cm) in height, so plant them near to the front of a border where their flowers can be seen easily

How to grow: Plant the bulbs in early spring 4in (10cm) deep in good, well-drained but not particularly rich soil. Space the bulbs about 6–8in (15–20cm) apart. A light dressing of a well-balanced fertilizer in the spring is beneficial. Water the plants well during any long, hot, dry periods

Flowering period: Mid-summer onwards

Maintenance: In mild districts the bulbs can be overwintered in the ground, otherwise it is a good idea to lift and store the bulbs in a dry, well-ventilated, frost-free place before the first frosts of autumn. Replant the bulbs early the following spring

Propagation: Remove small offsets, and grow these on in a nursery bed. They should reach flowering size in two to three years

Pests and diseases: The bulbs can fall victim to a fungus disease that produces a blue mould, and ultimately rotting of the bulbs

BELOW *Trillium grandiflorum*: known as wake robin

ABOVE *Trillium sessile*: left undisturbed it will build up into sizeable clumps

NAME: *TRILLIUM* (WAKE ROBIN, WOOD LILY)
FAMILY: **TRILLIACEAE**

Description: These hardy perennial plants produce rhizomes, and are native to North America. In spring a well-established clump of Trillium presents a splendid sight with its pure white flowers. These have three slightly reflexed petals on short 12in (30cm) stems. As they age, the blooms gradually become flushed with pink. Trilliums are not difficult to grow, in the right conditions. When established they will slowly form into sizeable clumps

Popular species and varieties: The best known is *Trillium grandiflorum* (AGM), often referred to as wake robin. It is mostly to be found growing in shady spots beneath deciduous trees. There is also a lovely double form 'Flore Pleno' (AGM), more expensive but a very desirable plant.

Another member of the family that always attracts attention is *T. sessile*. Its leaves are deep green, marbled and blotched with grey. The variable but usually maroon flowers are different from *T. grandiflorum*, being stemless, narrow, erect and pointed with slightly twisted petals. The stems are slightly shorter, at 10–12in (20–30cm), and are produced from late spring.

Occasionally, reference is made to *T. sessile* var. *luteum*; this should in fact read *T. luteum*. It has mottled foliage and very similar flowers, that have petals of greenish-yellow

Where to grow: Trilliums are woodland plants requiring cool, moist, humus-rich soil. Dappled shade provided by trees and shrubs is ideal

141

How to grow: Plant the rhizomes 3in (7.5cm) deep in late summer or early autumn. They are best in groups, with individuals spaced at 12in (30cm) apart. It is important that they do not dry out in the spring and summer months, watering is required in periods of hot, dry weather

Flowering period: Late spring to early summer

Maintenance: Remove dead foliage after the plants have died down. An annual dressing of well-rotted leaf mould or compost is beneficial in winter

Propagation: In late summer and early autumn, lift and carefully divide the rhizomes. Avoid the temptation to divide more than necessary, and ensure that each section retains at least one growing point. Replant the divisions immediately

Pests and diseases: The problem most likely to be encountered is that of slug damage, mainly to young shoots and flowers. Otherwise the plants are trouble-free

---

NAME: _TRITELIA_
FAMILY: ALLIACEAE

Description: These plants are native to California and can occasionally be found listed as _Brodiaea_; they have rich deep blue flowers. In many ways the corms resemble those of the crocus

Popular species and varieties: The large funnel-shaped blue flowers of _Tritelelia laxa_ are noted for their long-lasting qualities. Individual flowers measure 1in (2.5cm) across, and are held on wiry stems some 12–18in (30–45cm) tall. The best-known member of this family is _T. laxa_ 'Queen Fabiola', now more correctly known as 'Koningin Fabiola'. It is very similar to the species plants, except that its flowers are a deeper blue

BELOW _Tritelia laxa_ 'Koningin Fabiola': long-lasting rich blue flowers

ABOVE *Tulbaghia*: clump-forming, requires a sheltered spot

Where to grow: In an open, sunny position in light soil that, ideally, becomes dry in the summer months

How to grow: Plant in groups during autumn, at a depth of 2in (5cm), and spaced 3in (7.5cm) apart. The foliage is untidy and often turns brown during flowering, so it is a good idea to camouflage this with other, low-growing plants

Flowering period: Mid- to late spring

Maintenance: Remove dead foliage at the end of the season. Feeding is not normally required

Propagation: Lift the corms after flowering and remove offsets to grow on. Tritelias can also be grown from seed sown in the autumn, but they will take some time to reach flowering size

Pests and diseases: No problems generally

NAME: *TULBAGHIA* (WILD GARLIC)
FAMILY: ALLIACEAE

Description: These are plants that require a warm, sunny, sheltered position in the garden; they produce clumps of grassy foliage

Popular species and varieties: *Tulbaghia violacea* is the one most often seen in our gardens, with grey-green foliage and rose-violet flower heads held on stems 16in (40cm) high. When crushed, the foliage has a recognizable onion smell, typical of plants in this, the onion family

Where to grow: Select a warm spot where the growing plants are not subjected to cold winds

How to grow: Plant the bulbs in spring, 1in (2.5cm) deep and 6in (15cm) apart, in good humus-rich soil. These plants are vigorous and will, in time, form clumps that can become congested and require dividing

Flowering period: Flowers are produced for several weeks during the summer

Maintenance: Lift and divide when congested; tidy the site in the autumn. During the growing season, and particularly in hot, dry weather, keep the soil moist

Propagation: Divide the clumps during autumn, and replant the bulbs immediately

Pests and diseases: No problems generally

143

RIGHT *Tulipa kaufmanniana*: flowers in early spring

NAME: *TULIPA* (TULIP)
FAMILY: **LILIACEAE**

Description: Tulips, with their kaleidoscope of colours, shapes and sizes, are indispensable for brilliant displays. Among the first to flower are those from the Kaufmannia group; these brighten up our gardens in late winter, with others taking the display through to late spring.

Tulips were introduced to European gardens in the mid-16th century. 'Tulip mania' swept Holland later, with individual bulbs changing hands for colossal prices, until the bubble burst which resulted in tremendous losses for some people. Fortunately all this was a long time ago. Holland is world renowned for its tulips, with huge amounts of land given over for the growing and development of these very popular bulbs.

There are around 100 species, and many more named varieties, with new additions making their debut each year. Tulips are best planted in groups in beds or borders; they are also excellent for growing in tubs and patio containers. Few plants can match the range of colours, from brilliant scarlet through to delicate pastel shades and pure white.

Over the years much breeding work has been carried out on tulips, with types to suit most people. Heights vary, with some of the species no more than 4in (10cm) high; the stately Darwin hybrids and more graceful lily-flowered types are as high as 24in (60cm) high. There are also the flamboyant Parrot types, distinctive fringed types, multi-flowered types and the rather mysterious Viridifloras, their blooms having varying amounts of green in them.

Each year sees many thousands of visitors to the world-famous Keukenhof Gardens near Lisse in Holland, the showpiece of the Dutch bulb industry. The large gardens in their mature setting have huge displays many types of bulbous plant, but the tulips are by far and away the most spectacular

Popular species and varieties: The species have a particular charm. *Tulipa tarda* (AGM) is one of the most desirable, its white flowers

LEFT *Tulipa tarda*: ideal for front of borders or the rock garden

ABOVE *Tulipa praestans* 'Unicum': an old favourite

ABOVE *Tulipa* 'Red Riding Hood': a member of the Greigii group

having a bright yellow base. Growing to just 4in (10cm) makes this one best for the front of a border or in a sunny pocket on the rock garden. Slightly later flowering is *T. hageri*, its distinctive 4in (10cm) high flowers of a dull red overlaid with olive-green give it an overall curious greenish appearance.

T. linifolia (AGM) is a species you could hardly miss, with its cup-shaped, glowing scarlet flowers with their violet-black centres. This grows to 4in (10cm) and flowers in late spring, when many of the tulips are past their best.

Those who like unusual flowers will probably find *T. acuminata* to their liking. Growing to 18in (45cm), its scarlet and yellow blooms are long, and their narrow, tapering petals have an almost thread-like point.

One should not overlook the lady tulip, *T. clusiana*, which was first grown in Holland in the very early 1600s. In early spring it produces cherry-red outer petals, and inner white petals with a violet base. Also with a

ABOVE *Tulipa* 'Monte Carlo': one of the best double early yellow varieties

ABOVE *Tulipa* 'New Design': an attractive mid-season tulip

ABOVE *Tulipa* 'Apeldoorn' and 'Maytime': tulip beds at their finest

BELOW *Tulipa* 'Spring Green': one of the fascinating Viridiflora type

long history are *T. praestans* 'Fusilier' (AGM), bright red, and 'Unicum', best described as capsicum-red. Both have two to five flowers on 12in (30cm) high stems.

The *Kaufmannianas* are the earliest group o flower, starting in late winter. While the straightforward species, *T. kaufmanniana*, is available it is the named varieties that are best known. These are ideal for a sunny pocket on the rock garden, front of a border, a windowbox or patio container. Those to look out for include: 'Heart's Delight', ivory white, with the outside of their petals carmine-red, edged with pale rose; 'Scarlet Baby', a dazzling scarlet with a yellow base; and 'Concerto', white. Tulips in this group range in height from 5–8in (12–20cm).

At the beginning of spring the 'early single' tulips come into bloom. One of the best known is 'Couleur Cardinal', with a strong, erect habit, its plum-crimson blooms being held on 14in (35cm) high stems. 'Princess Irene' (AGM) is another popular variety and grows to the same height; its blooms are a lovely soft orange with purple flame-like marks arising from the base.

The 'early double' tulips include: 'Peach Blossom', deep rose (the flowers stand up well to windy weather), and 'Willemsoord', a distinctive variety with petals of carmine,

edged white. Both forms are good container varieties, and can be used for forcing.

Mid-spring is when the variegated-leaved 'Greigii' tulips – often referred to as the Peacock tulips – are at their best. There are some really outstanding varieties among them, ranging from the rich scarlet 'Red Riding Hood' (AGM) to the vermilion red, wavy edged 'Pinocchio', and lemon yellow tinged red 'Golden Day'.

The multi-flowered tulips create much interest in the garden, most growing to around 18in (45cm) in height, with three to six flowers on each stem. Two of the best are 'Georgette', a glistening clear yellow, and 'Red Georgette', a bright red.

The mid-season Darwin hybrids and May-flowering groups include some of the best tulips for beds and borders. You can find varieties with brilliant colours, while others have more delicate pastel shades. The Darwin hybrids have rounded flowers and are among the largest of all tulips. These are striking in beds and borders.

'Cassini' has a beautiful deep red flower, 'Negritta' is beetroot-purple and 'White Dream' is ivory-white. The latter also has good resistance to inclement weather. Describing some varieties is not easy, such as 'New Design': the outside of the petals is described as 'Naples yellow' fading to a pinkish white with a pale fuchsia red margin; the inside is yellow with apricot flame. 'Shirley' is another good variety; ivory-white with a narrow band of purple, the blooms are also lightly spotted.

Well known for its splendid displays is 'Golden Apeldoorn' a rich golden yellow with occasional red flecks. 'Holland's Glorie' (AGM) is a real beauty, with bright red flowers. Equally as good for its brilliant red blooms is 'Big Chief'

The May-flowering group includes 'Black Swan' (AGM), a deep velvety maroon-black that stands out particularly well among brighter colours, as does the delightful rose-pink

ABOVE *Tulipa* 'China Pink': an Award of Garden Merit holder of the Lily-flowered group

ABOVE *Tulipa* 'Flaming Frilled': an attractive member of the fringed tulips

ABOVE *Tulipa* 'Bing Crosby': a spectacular red Triumph tulip

'Menton', its blooms suffused with apricot-pink edges. These tulips have perfectly shaped flowers most on sturdy stems around 24in (60cm) in height.

The Lily-flowered tulips are unsurpassed for their elegance and charm. Most grow to around 20in (50cm) high, the blooms being easily recognizable by their reflexed petals. Among the best are the deep primrose yellow 'West Point' (AGM), the lovely pure white 'White Triumphator' (AGM) and the eye-catching 'Marilyn', an outstanding white with considerable feathering and flame markings of fuchsine purple.

Tulips in the Viridiflora group are splendid for bedding, and very popular with flower arrangers.

A feature of these varieties is that there is always an amount of green in their petals. One of the most outstanding is 'Spring Green' (AGM); its blooms are an ivory-white feathered with green, and it has light green anthers.

In mid-spring the Paeony-flowered tulips are in full bloom. Robust, and on sturdy 20in (50cm) stems, in many cases the double blooms are scented. One of the best is 'Allegretto', a deep red with narrow golden edge.

The Parrot tulip brings a touch of the exotic to any garden. 'Flamboyant' describes them well, with their showy fringed and scalloped petals, to say nothing of their sensational colours. One that never fails to attract attention is 'Giant Parrot', with vermilion-red blooms.

LEFT *Tulip* 'Daydream' (AGM) is one of the superb Darwin hybrids

any earlier and growth may take place, only to be damaged by the winter frosts. The larger types should be set 6in (15cm) deep and apart. Plant the smaller types, including the species, 4in (10cm) deep and apart. For the best effect set them out in groups in the border unless large planting schemes are planned

Flowering period: Depending on variety, from late winter to late spring

Maintenance: Tulips can be left in the ground for two or three years. Many people prefer to lift them, to make way for something else in the summer, and then replant in the autumn. This can be made easier by using bulb containers that are simply lifted after flowering and re-planted elsewhere in the garden. The dwarf types are usually left in the ground, especially if planted on the rock garden. In dry weather water the plants well, especially if the flower buds have appeared. Remove dead flower stems and foliage, once they have died, on any plants that are to remain in the ground

Propagation: Removal of offsets is best, and is the usual method of increasing stock. Grade them as the largest may well flower the following year; others will take longer. If you want a good display, for a certain occasion or position in the garden, you should plant new bulbs

Pests and diseases: Take care where you store tulip bulbs, as mice have a liking for them. Slugs can damage new growth; aphids can also be a problem at this time.

Virus diseases result in streaked, mottled and distorted foliage. Dig up and burn any affected plants.

Tulip fire is a fungal disease causing the foliage to be stunted, with dark blotches, and ultimately rotting of the bulbs; dig up and burn. Grey bulb rot is another fungal disease, again with no cure. The spores of these fungus diseases may remain in the soil, so it is best to avoid planting tulips in the same area

Neither could you miss the old favourite 'Flaming Parrot', a mixture of brilliant red and yellow. 'Apricot Parrot' (AGM) is a pale apricot-yellow, lightly tinged with cream-white and soft pink

Where to grow: Tulips are ideal for beds and borders, with the lower-growing varieties good for patio containers and windowboxes. Many of the species are splendid for the rock garden; in addition some are suitable for growing in a cool greenhouse

How to grow: The position chosen should be sunny, with some protection from the wind. Tulips enjoy alkaline, humus-rich soils. If the soil is acid, add lime a week or two before planting. This should take place in late autumn;

NAME: *WATSONIA*
FAMILY: **IRIDACEAE**

Description: These striking gladiolus-like plants are native to South Africa. They are tender and you should lift and store the corms in a frost-free place for the winter. Only in the very mildest districts are they likely to survive outside

Popular species and varieties: The variety most likely to be seen in our gardens is *Watsonia pillansii* (syn *W. beatricis*). It has narrow, erect foliage reaching 18–36in (45–90cm); the wiry flower stems carry up to 30 narrow, funnel-shaped orange-red blooms each about 3in (7.5cm) in length; the mouth of the flower is normally 1½in (4cm) across

Where to grow: Choose a sunny spot at the back of a sheltered, sunny border, or grow the corms in pots in a greenhouse

How to grow: Watsonias require light soil; other types should be improved by adding coarse sand or grit. Plant the corms during mid- to late spring, some 4in (10cm) deep and 12in (30cm) apart

Flowering period: Late spring to early summer

Maintenance: Remove dead flower stems. Lift the corms in the autumn, dry and store in a frost-free airy place until the spring

Propagation: Divide the corms, or grow from seed which can take three to five years to reach flowering size

Pests and diseases: Generally trouble-free

NAME: *ZANTEDESCHIA* (ARUM LILY)
FAMILY: **ARACEAE**

Description: The pure white waxy flowers of the arum lily add grace and charm to any garden. These rhizome-forming hardy perennials are native to South Africa. *Zantedeschia aethiopica* (AGM) is a moisture-lover and can be grown in mild districts in a sheltered position in a border, or as a marginal at the edge of a pond. Others are only suitable for a greenhouse or conservatory

Popular species and varieties: *Zantedeschia aethiopica* has glossy mid-green arrow-shaped leaves. The white spathes, with very distinctive yellow spadix are up to 8in (20cm) long; they appear in late spring and summer. The form 'Crowborough' (AGM) is generally regarded as the hardiest. One for milder areas, and which has greenish spathes, is 'Green Goddess' (AGM).

ABOVE *Watsonia pillansii*: dense spikes of up to 30 flowers

Two species that are widely offered are
Z. elliottiana, the golden arum lily with spotted
foliage, and *Z. rehmanii* (the pink arum). Both
can be grown outside during the summer
months but should be lifted and given
protection from frost during the winter

Where to grow: *Zantedeschia aethiopica* is
often grown as a marginal plant in ponds and
will survive most winters. It can also be grown
in shallow water that does not exceed 12in
(30cm) in depth. This lily is also successful in
a south-facing border, but plenty of water is
required during the summer

How to grow: Plant the rhizomes in spring,
6in (15cm) deep, and space them 18in (45cm)
apart. If grown under glass, planting can take
place in early spring, setting the rhizomes in 8in
(20cm) pots of John Innes no. 2 or a peat-based
compost. Cover the rhizomes with 3in (7.5cm)
of compost, water, and keep them just moist
until growth starts, at which time you should
increase the amount. Feed the plants in summer,
using a balanced liquid feed. As *Z. aethiopica*
finishes its flowering, gradually reduce the
amounts of water you apply. No water should
be given to the other species mentioned, after
they have died down

ABOVE *Zantedeschia* 'Crowborough' is regarded as the
hardiest of the well-known arum lilies

Flowering period: Late spring and summer
Maintenance: Remove flowers as they fade.
Z. aethiopica should be given a layer of straw
as protection during the winter, especially in
cold areas. Others need to be lifted and stored
under glass for the winter
Propagation: Divide the rhizomes after flowering
Pests and diseases: A fungal disease can
attack rhizomes, causing them to rot. It can
spread rapidly, so the best advice is to lift and
destroy the plants as soon as it is seen

ABOVE *Zantedeschia elliottiana* requires winter protection

Glossary

acid soil A soil that contains no free lime, with pH of less than 6.5

AGM The Award of Garden Merit – an award given to plants having exceptionally good garden qualities, presented by the Royal Horticultural Society

alkaline Soils where lime is present

axil The junction of leaf and stem joint

basal A shoot emerging from neck or crown of a plant

blotched Petals with irregularly scattered colour patches

bone meal A fertilizer made from ground animal bone

boss Prominent centre stamens

bulb General term used for bulbs, corms, tubers and rhizomes

bulbil A small bulb produced on a leaf joint and stem of some mature bulbous plants

cold frame An unheated box with sides of wood, plastic or brick, and which has a removable transparent top, used to protect plants from the cold

corm A storage organ that does not have scales

corolla A term used to describe the six petals on a daffodil

cultivar Cultivated variety

dead heading Removal of dead flowers

division Dividing a plant; a form of propagation

falls A term used to describe the outer petals of *Iris*

fungicide Chemical product used to control fungal diseases

germination The development of seed into seedlings

ground cover Low-growing plants

grow on Leave to grow until of a size suitable for planting out

half hardy Plants that cannot survive winter outside

heavy soil Soil containing a high proportion of clay

humus Organic matter in soil

hybrid A plant raised from two species, varieties or cultivars

insecticide Chemical product used to control insect pests

leaf mould Decomposed leaves, used to improve soil

liquid feed Fertilizer in liquid form, used diluted

move on Transferring a plant to its permanent position

mulch Bulky organic matter applied around plants to conserve moisture and deter weed growth

naturalize Plants growing as in the wild; being allowed to colonize

nutrient deficiency Problems due to lack of essential elements in the soil

pendent Flowers or leaves that hang down

perennial Plants that grow and flower year after year

pesticide Chemical products used to control insect or animal pests

pH Measure of acidity

plant out To plant into a permanent, flowering position

prepared bulbs Specially treated bulbs for early flowering indoors

prick out To remove seedlings from the pot or tray and space them into other trays to allow an increase in size

propagator Item of equipment used for raising seedlings or rooting cuttings

reflexed Petals that are bent back

scaling The term used in the propagation of lily bulbs

self-seeding A plant that scatters its seed naturally, indoors or outside

spawn The term used to describe bulblets

systemic Pesticide (including fungicides) that is absorbed by the plant and travels through the plant in the sap flow

tender Plants liable to frost damage

transplant Moving a plant from one place to another

trumpet Cup or corona in the centre of a daffodil flower

tuber Underground storage organ

tunic Fibrous membrane covering some bulbs

umbel Type of flower head: umbrella shaped

variegated Leaves that are blotched, spotted or edged with a different colour

virus Organism for which there is no cure, causing malformation and discoloration of affected plants

About the author

Plants have played a major part in Eric Sawford's life, even from before his school days – his father worked as a head gardener. At the tender ago of 16 his sizeable and comprehensive collection of cushion-forming alpine saxifrages attracted the attention of the local newspaper, and were even featured on the front page.

When Eric left school he worked for well-known nurserymen Wood & Ingram, until he was called up for National Service with the RAF. Back in civvy street he returned to gardening and, although he continued working with plants, he also gained professional experience with seeds, garden machinery and many other types of gardening products.

Over the years he has grown numerous types of plants, including bulbs, shrubs, hardy perennials, fuchias and alpines (the latter to show standard, with more than a little success).

In the 1970s Eric began photographing plants and gardens. Wherever possible, he takes pictures of plants growing in their natural habitat, including alpines in the Alps and other subjects in warmer climates. As a result, he has built up an extensive photographiuc library; his fabulous pictures can be seen in numerous books, as well as the hundreds of features he has written for the national gardening press.

Index

Pages highlighted in **bold** include illustrations of plants

Titles available from
GMC Publications Books

GARDENING

Alpine Gardening	Chris & Valerie Wheeler
Auriculas for Everyone: How to Grow and Show Perfect Plants	Mary Robinson
Beginners' Guide to Herb Gardening	Yvonne Cuthbertson
Beginners' Guide to Water Gardening	Graham Clarke
Big Leaves for Exotic Effect	Stephen Griffith
Companions to Clematis: Growing Clematis with Other Plants	Marigold Badcock
Creating Contrast with Dark Plants	Freya Martin
Creating Small Habitats for Wildlife in your Garden	Josie Briggs
Exotics are Easy	GMC Publications
Gardening with Hebes	Chris & Valerie Wheeler
Gardening with Shrubs	Eric Sawford
Gardening with Wild Plants	Julian Slatcher
Growing Cacti and Other Succulents in the Conservatory and Indoors	Shirley-Anne Bell
Growing Cacti and Other Succulents in the Garden	Shirley-Anne Bell
Growing Successful Orchids in the Greenhouse and Conservatory	Mark Isaac-Williams
Hardy Palms and Palm-Like Plants	Martyn Graham
Hardy Perennials: A Beginner's Guide	Eric Sawford
Hedges: Creating Screens and Edges	Averil Bedrich
How to Attract Butterflies to your Garden	John & Maureen Tampion
Marginal Plants	Bernard Sleeman
Orchids are Easy: A Beginner's Guide to their Care and Cultivation	Tom Gilland
Planting Plans for Your Garden	Jenny Shukman
Sink and Container Gardening Using Dwarf Hardy Plants	Chris & Valerie Wheeler
The Successful Conservatory and Growing Exotic Plants	Joan Phelan
Success with Bulbs	Eric Sawford
Success with Cuttings	Chris & Valerie Wheeler
Success with Seeds	Chris & Valerie Wheeler
Tropical Garden Style with Hardy Plants	Alan Hemsley
Water Garden Projects: From Groundwork to Planting	Roger Sweetinburgh

WOODWORKING

Beginning Picture Marquetry	Lawrence Threadgold
Carcass Furniture	GMC Publications
Celtic Carved Lovespoons: 30 Patterns	Sharon Littley & Clive Griffin
Celtic Woodcraft	Glenda Bennett
Celtic Woodworking Projects	Glenda Bennett
Complete Woodfinishing (Revised Edition)	Ian Hosker
David Charlesworth's Furniture-Making Techniques	David Charlesworth
David Charlesworth's Furniture-Making Techniques – Volume 2	David Charlesworth
Furniture Projects with the Router	Kevin Ley
Furniture Restoration (Practical Crafts)	Kevin Jan Bonner
Furniture Restoration: A Professional at Work	John Lloyd
Furniture Workshop	Kevin Ley
Green Woodwork	Mike Abbott
History of Furniture: Ancient to 1900	Michael Huntley
Intarsia: 30 Patterns for the Scrollsaw	John Everett
Making Heirloom Boxes	Peter Lloyd
Making Screw Threads in Wood	Fred Holder
Making Woodwork Aids and Devices	Robert Wearing
Mastering the Router	Ron Fox
Pine Furniture Projects for the Home	Dave Mackenzie
Router Magic: Jigs, Fixtures and Tricks to Unleash your Router's Full Potential	Bill Hylton
Router Projects for the Home	GMC Publications
Router Tips & Techniques	Robert Wearing
Routing: A Workshop Handbook	Anthony Bailey
Routing for Beginners (Revised and Expanded Edition)	Anthony Bailey
Stickmaking: A Complete Course	Andrew Jones & Clive George
Stickmaking Handbook	Andrew Jones & Clive George
Storage Projects for the Router	GMC Publications
Success with Sharpening	Ralph Laughton
Veneering: A Complete Course	Ian Hosker
Veneering Handbook	Ian Hosker
Wood: Identification & Use	Terry Porter
Woodworking Techniques and Projects	Anthony Bailey
Woodworking with the Router: Professional Router Techniques any Woodworker can Use	Bill Hylton & Fred Matlack

CRAFTS

Bargello: A Fresh Approach to Florentine Embroidery	Brenda Day
Bead and Sequin Embroidery Stitches	Stanley Levy
Beginning Picture Marquetry	Lawrence Threadgold
Blackwork: A New Approach	Brenda Day
Celtic Backstitch	Helen Hall
Celtic Cross Stitch Designs	Carol Phillipson
Celtic Knotwork Designs	Sheila Sturrock
Celtic Knotwork Handbook	Sheila Sturrock
Celtic Spirals and Other Designs	Sheila Sturrock
Celtic Spirals Handbook	Sheila Sturrock
Complete Pyrography	Stephen Poole
Creating Made-to-Measure Knitwear: A Revolutionary Approach to Knitwear Design	Sylvia Wynn
Creative Backstitch	Helen Hall
Creative Log-Cabin Patchwork	Pauline Brown
Creative Machine Knitting	GMC Publications
Cross-Stitch Designs from China	Carol Phillipson
Cross-Stitch Designs from India	Carol Phillipson
Cross-Stitch Floral Designs	Joanne Sanderson
Cross-Stitch Gardening Projects	Joanne Sanderson
Decoration on Fabric: A Sourcebook of Ideas	Pauline Brown
Decorative Beaded Purses	Enid Taylor
Designing and Making Cards	Glennis Gilruth
Designs for Pyrography and Other Crafts	Norma Gregory
Dried Flowers: A Complete Guide	Lindy Bird
Easy Wedding Planner	Jenny Hopkin

159

Exotic Textiles in Needlepoint	Stella Knight
Glass Engraving Pattern Book	John Everett
Glass Painting	Emma Sedman
Handcrafted Rugs	Sandra Hardy
Hand-Dyed Yarn Craft Projects	Debbie Tomkies
Hobby Ceramics: Techniques and Projects for Beginners	Patricia A. Waller
How to Arrange Flowers: A Japanese Approach to English Design	Taeko Marvelly
How to Make First-Class Cards	Debbie Brown
An Introduction to Crewel Embroidery	Mave Glenny
Machine-Knitted Babywear	Christine Eames
Making Fabergé-Style Eggs	Denise Hopper
Making Fairies and Fantastical Creatures	Julie Sharp
Making Hand-Sewn Boxes: Techniques and Projects	Jackie Woolsey
Making Kumihimo: Japanese Interlaced Braids	Rodrick Owen
Making Mini Cards, Gift Tags & Invitations	Glennis Gilruth
Making Polymer Clay Cards and Tags	Jacqui Eccleson
Making Wirecraft Cards	Kate MacFadyen
Native American Bead Weaving	Lynne Garner
New Ideas for Crochet: Stylish Projects for the Home	Darsha Capaldi
Paddington Bear in Cross-Stitch	Leslie Hills
Papercraft Projects for Special Occasions	Sine Chesterman
Papermaking and Bookbinding: Coastal Inspirations	Joanne Kaar
Patchwork for Beginners	Pauline Brown
Pyrography Designs	Norma Gregory
Rose Windows for Quilters	Angela Besley
Silk Painting for Beginners	Jill Clay
Sponge Painting	Ann Rooney
Stained Glass: Techniques and Projects	Mary Shanahan
Step-by-Step Card Making	Glennis Gilruth
Step-by-Step Pyrography Projects for the Solid Point Machine	Norma Gregory
Stitched Cards and Gift Tags for Special Occasions	Carol Phillipson
Tassel Making for Beginners	Enid Taylor
Tatting Collage	Lindsay Rogers
Tatting Patterns	Lyn Morton
Temari: A Traditional Japanese Embroidery Technique	Margaret Ludlow

Three-Dimensional Découpage: Innovative Projects for Beginners	Hilda Stokes
Trompe l'Oeil: Techniques and Projects	Jan Lee Johnson
Tudor Treasures to Embroider	Pamela Warner
Wax Art	Hazel Marsh

PHOTOGRAPHY

Close-Up on Insects	Robert Thompson
Digital Enhancement for Landscape Photographers	Arjan Hoogendam & Herb Parkin
Double Vision	Chris Weston & Nigel Hicks
An Essential Guide to Bird Photography	Steve Young
Field Guide to Bird Photography	Steve Young
Field Guide to Landscape Photography	Peter Watson
How to Photograph Pets	Nick Ridley
In my Mind's Eye: Seeing in Black and White	Charlie Waite
Life in the Wild: A Photographer's Year	Andy Rouse
Light in the Landscape: A Photographer's Year	Peter Watson
Photographers on Location with Charlie Waite	Charlie Waite
Photographing Wilderness	Jason Friend
Photographing your Garden	Gail Harland
Photography for the Naturalist	Mark Lucock
Photojournalism: An Essential Guide	David Herrod
Professional Landscape and Environmental Photography: From 35mm to Large Format	Mark Lucock
Rangefinder	Roger Hicks & Frances Schultz
Underwater Photography	Paul Kay
Where and How to Photograph Wildlife	Peter Evans
Wildlife Photography Workshops	Steve & Ann Toon

ART TECHNIQUES

Beginning Watercolours	Bee Morrison
Oil Paintings from the Landscape: A Guide for Beginners	Rachel Shirley
Oil Paintings from your Garden: A Guide for Beginners	Rachel Shirley
Sketching Landscapes in Pen and Pencil	Joyce Percival

MAGAZINES

WOODTURNING ● WOODCARVING ● FURNITURE & CABINETMAKING ● THE ROUTER
NEW WOODWORKING ● THE DOLLS' HOUSE MAGAZINE ● OUTDOOR PHOTOGRAPHY
BLACK & WHITE PHOTOGRAPHY ● KNITTING ● GUILD NEWS

The above represents a selection of the titles currently published or scheduled to be published.
All are available direct from the Publishers or through bookshops, newsagents and specialist retailers.
To place an order, or to obtain a complete catalogue, contact:

GMC Publications,
Castle Place, 166 High Street, Lewes, East Sussex BN7 1XU United Kingdom
Tel: 01273 488005 Fax: 01273 402866
E-mail: pubs@thegmcgroup.com
Website: www.gmcbooks.com
Orders by credit card are accepted